More than a Page

Irresistible Paper Crafts and the Pages That Inspired Them

Tina has always been a very beautiful child. As I have watched her grow and mature, I am struck not only by her beauty on the outside but also the inner beauty and strength developing within her soul. The sparkle that shines through her eyes with each smile seems to come straight from the heart. She truly is a natural beauty!

Tina

Natural Beauty

Love

From the Editors of Memory Makers Books, Denver, Colorado

Managing Editor MaryJo Regier

Editor Jodi Amidei

Art Director Nick Nyffeler

Photographer Ken Trujillo

Art Acquisitions Editor Janetta Abucejo Wieneke

Graphic Designers Jordan Kinney, Robin Rozum

Administrative Assistant Karen Cain

Editorial Support Amy Glander, Emily Curry Hitchingham

Contributing Writer Torrey Scott

Contributing Photographers Camillo DiLizia, Jennifer Reeves

Copy Editor Dena Twinem

Contributing Memory Makers Masters Kathy Fesmire, Nicola Howard, Torrey Scott, Shannon Taylor

Production Coordinator Matthew Wagner

Published by Memory Makers Books, an imprint of F+W Publications, Inc.
12365 Huron Street, Suite 500, Denver, CO 80234
Phone (800) 254-9124
First edition. Printed in the United States.
10 09 08 07 06 5 4 3 2 1

Library of Congress Cataloging-in-Publication Data

More than a page : irresistible paper crafts and the pages that inspired them / from the editors of
    Memory Makers Books.-- 1st ed.
        p. cm
    Includes index.
    ISBN-13: 978-1-892127-86-0
    ISBN-10: 1-892127-86-5
    1. Paper work. I. Memory Makers Books.

TT870.M58 2006
745.54--dc22

2006042017

Distributed to trade and art markets by
F+W Publications, Inc.
4700 East Galbraith Road, Cincinnati, OH 45236
Phone (800) 289-0963

Distributed in Canada by
Fraser Direct
100 Armstrong Avenue
Georgetown, ON, Canada L7G 5S4
Tel: (905) 877-4411

Distributed in the U.K. and Europe by
David & Charles
Brunel House, Newton Abbot,
Devon, TQ12 4PU, England
Tel: (+44) 1626 323200, Fax: (+44) 1626 323319
E-mail: mail@davidandcharles.co.uk

Distributed in Australia by
Capricorn Link
P.O. Box 704, S. Windsor NSW, 2756 Australia
Tel: (02) 4577-3555

Memory Makers Books is the home of Memory Makers, the scrapbook magazine dedicated to educating and inspiring scrapbookers. To subscribe, or for more information, call (800) 366-6465. Visit us on the Internet at www.memorymakersmagazine.com.

We dedicate this book to the accomplished design team members whose talents continue to inspire and amaze us. We appreciate their innovation, creativity and abilities to produce such astonishing layouts and paper crafts.

Table of Contents

Showcasing springtime memories on beautiful and endearing scrapbook pages complemented by innovative and fantastic paper crafts

Bringing favorite summertime themes to life on fabulous and outstanding scrapbook layouts including many inspiring and eye-catching arts and crafts

Autumn in the Colorado Rocky Mountains is like no other season. The coolness of winter just moments away, but the warmth of summer still lingers during the daytime. The perfect combination of weather for a long hike to remote mountain peaks for spectacular views such as this one just another reason why I love living here!

Splendor

giggles

Smile

This was a great afternoon and a very fun photo shoot. You got the giggles and once they started, they were impossible to stop. Before too long you had us all laughing. It made for a great opportunity to get some extremely natural and lively smiles from you. That's one reason I love this photo so much. I love the way it makes me feel when I remember the sound of your giggles - such a precious sound to a mother's ears.

Giggle

Laugh

Introduction

It happens every time I've just completed a scrapbook page: I'm left staring at my work space—with all the remnants, unused portions of supplies and paper scraps just screaming for something to be done with them. So, I have two choices. I can clean up and put away all of these items or I can keep the creative flow going. Now that's really no choice at all if you ask me. Anyone who has ever scrapbooked with me will tell you that I'm no quitter; I'll keep going every time. And why not? After all, the color choices have all been made, the embellishments are all chosen and the design inspiration is still at my fingertips. There's no better time to create yet another work of art.

Whether it's a greeting card to share with a dear friend or a mini photo album to give to an ever-so-proud grandmother, now is the time to stretch my creativity and my scrapbooking supplies into something more—something beyond the scrapbook page.

In this book, I challenged eight top-industry artists to take this concept to heart. I had them create one astounding scrapbook page, but not quit there. I asked them to create two or three different paper crafts using the leftover supplies. I was amazed at what they came up with. I believe you, too, will be inspired by the treasure trove of wonderful ideas and projects the artists share within this book.

As you ponder the fabulous artwork contained in the following pages, I would challenge you to let your creative synergy see beyond your scrapbooks and into the world of paper crafts. Think of all the possibilities waiting for you after you have scrapbooked your latest cherished memory. Remember the friend who would appreciate the handmade card just waiting to be crafted. Or that dollar-store frame that just needs a little something extra to make it a treasured keepsake. The possibilities are endless if you just open your mind as you open these pages. I think if you test this concept, you just might become a "never say quit" type of scrapbooker...just like me!

Jodi

Jodi Amidei
Craft Editor
Memory Makers Books

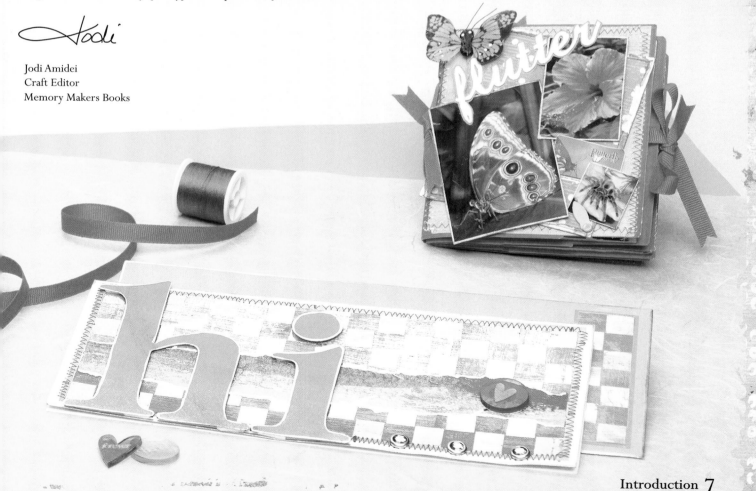

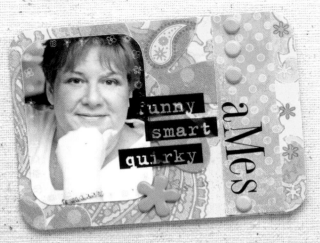

Amy ("Ames") Goldstein lives in Kent Lakes, New York. By day, she is the technical project manager/recruiter for several Fortune 100 companies. By night, she is Mom to two wonderful girls. She is married to Jeffrey and they also share their house with two dogs, three cats and a partridge in a pear tree. She started scrapbooking about two years ago and was immediately addicted. Amy describes herself as a "huge hoarder" who loves to involve people in her addiction.

Kathy Fesmire is an art teacher and freelance artist living in Athens, Tennessee, with her husband, four children and two dogs. She has been scrapbooking for eight years and in 2004 was named a Memory Makers Master. She has been on several product design teams and is currently working for one of the largest scrapbook product manufacturers in the world. She loves using bold and bright colors and strives to use her art background to incorporate the elements and principles of design into her layouts.

Together with her husband, Paul, and three children, Nic Howard lives in Pukekohe, New Zealand—outside of Auckland. She is a busy stay-at-home mum. She began scrapbooking seven years ago after perusing scrapbooking sites on the Internet. She's been hooked ever since. Nic says she spends five to six hours per night scrapbooking. Nic's passion paid off as she was named Memory Makers Master in 2005. When she's not scrapbooking, Nic enjoys spending time with her family and friends and "pottering outside" in her garden.

Heather Preckel started scrapbooking about seven years ago and says she has grown to love it more and more every day. She came onto the publishing scene three years ago and has enjoyed sharing her pages with readers ever since. Heather calls the western part of North Carolina home, in a town called Swannanoa. She lives with her husband and their 6-year-old daughter—both of whom, Heather says, are inspirations for her pages. Besides scrapbooking, she loves to read, cook and just spend time with her family.

Tricia Rubens started scrapbooking over three years ago when she found an idea book that "blew her socks off." She's married to her high-school sweetheart, Scott, and together they have two children. She loves to scrapbook everyday life–the good, the bad and the funny. When not scrapbooking, she is a marketing manager for a medical-equipment manufacturer, traveling the world speaking to promote blood donations to save patients' lives. She lives south of Denver in Castle Rock, Colorado. Born and raised in Wisconsin, Tricia proclaims she's still a "Cheesehead" at heart.

Torrey Scott jumped into scrapbooking six years ago and hasn't "come up for air" since. She describes it as "the conduit for my creative muse that keeps me sane." Torrey was a Memory Makers Masters in 2003. Married to Scotty, she describes him as a "wonderful man who supports my obsession." They are owned by a cat named Cosmo and live in Thornton, Colorado. Torrey recently retired from her 20-year career as a registered nurse. What's in store for Torrey now? She is looking to spread her creative wings and fly.

Shannon Taylor can't believe she's been scrapbooking for five years. She says, "It feels like it's been part of my life so much longer and I love that." She has been published nearly 300 times. Shannon was named a Memory Makers Master in 2005 and has won the title of *Creating Keepsakes Hall of Fame.* Shannon states, "I honestly never thought such amazing things would happen when I first picked up a pair of scrapbooking scissors. I'm so grateful." Shannon lives with her husband and two sons in Bristol, Tennessee.

Courtney Walsh is married to Adam, a children's pastor, and has two children. She says her life is "all about kids" and she loves every second! Courtney started scrapbooking to organize her photos and as an outlet for her writing. She admits scrapbooking rapidly spiraled into an obsession. She and her husband write plays and musicals and have had a few published. In her limited spare time, she loves to go to the movies. Courtney and her family call Winnebago, Illinois, home.

Getting Started

Whether you are a novice scrapbook enthusiast or a seasoned pro who has been scrapbooking for years, there will almost always be leftover supplies after the creation of a scrapbook layout. Chances are good that all those scraps are coordinated and have been chosen for certain color combinations, an exact theme or with a specific design in mind. This is the perfect time to take advantage of the fact that you are not starting from scratch. You have a color scheme and you have your supplies already in front of you with most of the time-consuming design choices already made. So, when the scrapbook page has been safely stored in that precious album, it's time to venture into the world of paper crafts.

Using This Method of Scrapbooking

This book will show you great ways to keep the creativity flowing far beyond the scrapbook page. Start simply by choosing a less complicated paper craft project for the first time around. You'll soon discover how easy it can be to create beautiful, one-of-a-kind pieces of art.

Card-making is a great choice for the beginning paper crafter. It will help you ease into this process. It doesn't take more than a few small scraps to decorate a blank card that creates a simple, handmade and thoughtful gift.

Or try transforming a plain spiral-bound notebook into a useful piece of art. Decorate the cover with small pieces of cardstock, some ribbon strips and suddenly you have a wonderful conversation piece to carry into your next meeting. Before you know it, you'll be creating fabulous home décor, amazing gift boxes and adorable mini-albums begging to be given to a special loved one.

With all this in mind, it's time to discover what potential the remnants of your scrapbook projects have and how easily they can become a treasured keepsake or one-of-a-kind gift to enjoy for years to come.

Supplies to Have on Hand

Try keeping a small stash of alterable objects on hand so that when the creative synergy is flowing, you've got all you need to keep the creative process going. Here are some examples of the type of things you might want to have waiting for your inspiration.

- blank cards
- blank envelopes
- blank tag shapes
- brown paper sacks
- CD cases
- checkbook covers
- children's board books
- chipboard pieces
- cigar boxes
- clipboards
- composition books
- frames
- gift bags
- jewelry boxes
- jewelry findings
- mint tins
- note holders
- notepads
- paint cans
- papier-mâché boxes
- papier-mâché shapes
- spiral-bound notebooks
- unused CDs
- wooden boxes
- wooden plaques

SPRING

Spring promises the freshness of a lively start, the growth of all that is alive, the warmth of the sunshine and new perspectives on life. Each delicate spring bud that raises its head to the sky is a sign that winter has left and that another season is upon us. Spring takes us outdoors, exploring the world with a keen sense of wonder. We celebrate our moms, our beliefs and new births. We watch as blooms spread, gardens grow and life is once again renewed. The pages and art in this chapter were designed specifically to inspire you to start fresh and fill your albums with all the wonder that comes with each spring season.

In the high mountaintops of Colorado, you can always count on the beautiful and delicate Columbine to assure you spring is on the way. While their petals are fragile and bruise easily, they are a very hearty plant that can withstand the frost that often softly kissed them each spring morning. They bring with them the promise of milden temperatures and days filled with the warm light of sunshine.

Blossom *Fresh* by Nic

Spring is a time for flowers! Take the opportunity to use your paper flowers from your layout and use them again to give a breath of spring to a picture frame, a notecard holder and a greeting card.

Supplies: Patterned paper (Chatterbox); acrylic letters (Heidi Swapp); paper flowers (Prima); preservation spray (Krylon); crackle medium, paper paint (Plaid); decorative brads (Queen & Co.); trim (source unknown); latex spray paint; notecard holder, cardstock

Early spring blossoms are always a welcome sight. These blossoms on the plum tree at Mum & Dads house are a welcome indication that warmer weather is on its way.

Visions of Spring

Soft pastel pinks and greens herald the coming of spring and provide the perfect platform for Nic's photo of cherry blossoms. Lightly stencil a floral image across the bottom of the photo. Use ribbons, decorative brads and silk flowers to repeat the pattern of the flowers in the photo, tying everything together in a beautiful package.

Stitched frame

Sew mitered strips of patterned-paper remnants from the page's journaling block to handcut cardstock frame. Gently curl edges of paper strips, ink edges with pen and affix to the front of the frame. Adhere leftover ribbon, trim, paper flowers and brads to the front of the frame. Personalize the frame with a handcut name from cardstock and adhere to the frame as a finishing touch.

Nic's tip:

Look around the house for reusable or alterable items like this notecard holder and frame to decorate with your leftover supplies. They make great bases for creating handmade keepsakes.

Embellished memo box

Paint wooden box, inside and out, with acrylic paint and crackle medium according to manufacturer's directions. When paint is dry, adhere matted, sewn strips of patterned-paper scraps to all sides. Add printed quote strip on top of box. Decorate with paper flowers, brads and paper bow. Glue rickrack around sides of box to complete.

Get-well card and envelope

Ink edges of patterned-paper rectangle scraps from page background and sew to cardstock mat. Ink edges of mat, wrap with ribbon and rickrack and adhere to card front. Affix acrylic letters to card front. Glue handcut cardstock words over acrylic letters. Finish with paper flower and brad. For envelope, ink edges of patterned-paper strips and sew onto cardstock mat. Add rickrack trim and sewn nameplate to envelope front.

Floral *Fancy*

We're all doodlers at heart, so why not apply these talents to your paper crafting? With pen in hand, journaling takes on a very personal feel and doodled elements add just the right touch to layouts and paper crafts of all kinds.

Supplies: Patterned paper (Chatterbox); decorative clip (EK Success); flower stamps (Wendi Speciale Designs); acrylic letters (Heidi Swapp); ribbons (Li'l Davis Designs, May Arts); snap-close spiral notebook (Target); cardstock; candy tin; card and envelope

Flower Picking

Heather carries the warm colors of nature, prominent in her photos, throughout the layout by her choice of patterned papers and embellishments. Use small photos to create an interesting border along the edge of the page. Use an oversized photo to establish the focal point for the layout. Mount handwritten subtitle and journaling to give the page a relaxed, natural, "country" feel.

Heather's tip:

Apply leftover page remnants to empty candy tins and small spiral notebooks to create fun mini projects and albums.

Birthday card and envelope

Carry the nature theme onto a whimsical card by cutting strips of patterned-paper scraps and adhere to card diagonally. Cut off excess as needed. Stamp butterfly image onto cardstock and cut out. Affix to card, adding decorative clip and ribbon for butterfly body. Write greeting on cardstock, mat on black and adhere to card front. Decorate envelope with stamped image, pen-work and handwritten "to" and "from" tags.

Tin album

Accordion-fold cardstock strip sized to fit into tin. Trim photos to page size and adhere to accordion pages. Adhere small, looped ribbon tab to front page. Affix backside of last accordion page to inside of tin bottom. Adhere completed journaling block to inside lid of tin. Decorate top and sides of tin with diagonally cut patterned paper, journaling strips and other embellishments as desired.

Mini spiral notebook

Adhere patterned paper to front and back cover. Affix ribbon down left side of front cover. Decorate patterned-paper square with stamped image and white ink pen. Adhere to front cover. Tie ribbon to snap tab to finish.

Easter *Joy*

by Shannon

Load an Easter layout with beautiful springtime ribbons of all patterns and styles. Then use them again to add spice on a fun Easter basket and unique card set.

Supplies: Patterned papers, letter stickers (Chatterbox); ribbons (American Crafts, Michaels); decorative clip, photo corner (Nunn Design); eyelet trim, letter buttons (Junkitz); basket (Michaels); decoupage medium (Plaid); burlap; card and envelope; CD; cardstock

The bunny, yup the bunny, was a major necessity for Easter this year. We went to buy some presents for little Elijah when Oliver made the claim that he really, really wanted & needed this little bunny! My little guy doesn't normally spend his evenings hugging on stuffed animals nor does he drag any around & he never has. But something about this white fuzzy bunny made my boy beg until he could beg no more! Did I flat out buy it for him? No. Did I sneak it above a magazine to the checkout counter to pay without him knowing it? You bet! He was so bummed out. But on Easter Day, when he found that little bunny amongst his goodies, his smile lit up my whole life. And now, months later, that little bunny is completely grungy. He's been loved. Oliver-2005

The Bunny

Shannon's page is warm, cuddly and full of rich colors and textures that translate well to additional paper crafts. Layer brightly colored woven ribbons over burlap to create an eye-catching backdrop for a cute-as-a-bunny layout. Use the eyelets in the ribbon as a platform for tying on additional ribbon elements. Adhere letter stickers for a simple yet effective title.

Easter basket

Affix strips of patterned paper to premade chipboard basket form. Coat with several layers of decoupage medium to bond, drying between each layer. Drill holes around top of basket. Tie ribbons through drilled holes. Glue burlap strip and ribbons around body of basket. Adhere letter stickers to front to complete.

CD card and envelope

Cover front and back of CD with patterned paper, making certain to cut out center hole. Adhere tied ribbon through center hole in spoke pattern around one-half of the CD. Affix letter stickers over ribbons, add photo corner and letter buttons to decorate. Hand-write message on remaining half of CD. Decorate the accompanying tag board CD holder with patterned paper, cardstock and ribbon to create a custom envelope.

Hunting *Fun* by Kathy

Wooden tags and flowers are often sold in bunches. So, once you've started, why not decorate the whole batch? You'll have plenty all ready to adorn your layout and paper crafts like a mini album and magnet set.

Supplies: Patterned papers (Bo-Bunny Press, K & Company); letter stickers (American Crafts, Bo-Bunny Press); rub-on letters (Making Memories); wooden flowers, numbers (Li'l Davis Designs); ribbons (Offray); rickrack (Wrights); decoupage medium (Plaid); wooden tags (source unknown); silk flowers; buttons; embroidery floss; cardstock; acrylic paint

Easter Egg Hunt

On Kathy's layout, the wonder of simple things shines through the eyes of a child and through colors as fun and playful as she. Create a collage of stickers, rub-on letters, buttons, ribbons, silk flowers and tags to form a delightfully eclectic title. Tuck ribbon-adorned journaling into an embellished library pocket to complete page.

Mini album

Cut four pieces of double-sided patterned paper from page remnants. Stack together and adhere strip of folded paper around one end of stack. Punch two holes through all layers and secure with tied ribbon for binding. Decorate pages of book with photos, handwritten sentiments on strips of patterned paper, wooden tags, ribbon, buttons and silk flowers. Add a sticker and rub-on letter title to finish the book. In similar fashion, decorate a library-style pocket made from patterned paper to house the book.

Wooden magnets

Print names onto different patterned-paper scraps and use to cover wooden tags. Add wooden flowers, ribbons and silk flowers. Glue decorated tags to magnets.

Kathy's tip:

Use up random sticker and rub-on letter odds and ends to create "ransom" style titles and page embellishments as done on the scrapbook page to the left.

Mother*Love*

by Torrey

Polymer clay is an incredibly versatile medium that allows you to create your own personalized accents for layouts. While you're at it, bake up a few extras to use on decorative boxes, cards and even jewelry!

Supplies: Patterned paper, letter stickers (Basic Grey); polymer clay (Eberhard Faber); foam stamps (Making Memories); mold (AMACO); pigment powder (Ranger); ribbon (Michaels); decorative scissors (Fiskars); star box (Hobby Lobby); jewelry findings (Darice); cardstock; vellum; stamping ink

Mom

Torrey designs an artistic tribute to her mother, the artist, for Mother's Day. Crop and layer photo duplicates in a unique manner. Create handmade polymer-clay sun accents (see jewelry caption on the next page for details on making polymer suns). Use the curved diagonal line of the patterned paper to create an unusual inner border to effectively set off the photo. Stamp architectural elements on background paper for depth and dimension. Make a simple title from letter stickers to add just the right finish.

Torrey's tip:

Create your own patterned paper using rubber or foam stamps on plain or patterned paper to add depth and dimension to your designs as done on the page at left.

Star-shaped gift box

Start with an unfinished wooden star-shaped box. Cover the top of the lid and sides of the box with contrasting leftover patterned papers. Apply ink to raw edges of box and lid. Affix ribbon around edge of lid. To complete, glue polymer clay sun elements to lid top.

Mother's Love card and envelope

Start with a cardstock card base and cover the front with patterned-paper scraps. Mat letter stickers on cardstock. Print sentiment onto vellum and adhere to card. Affix ribbon across card and adhere sticker word to ribbon. Glue polymer clay sun elements on card (see jewelry caption for details on making polymer suns). Ink edges of card and envelope. Affix patterned paper strip and ribbon to envelope to decorate.

Sun earrings and brooch

Make the polymer clay sun elements by rolling clay into small balls and pressing firmly into mold. Carefully remove from mold and trim away excess. Gently rub pigment powder on high points of sun. Make hand-rolled beads from clay. Pierce hole through suns and beads prior to baking. Bake according to manufacturer's directions. Assemble earrings using premade headpins and earring loops. For brooch, cut strips of patterned paper and ink edges. Glue paper strips to back of large sun and affix pin back.

Mother's *Luck* by Nic

Supplies: Patterned papers (Autumn Leaves, Urban Lily); acrylic shapes (Heidi Swapp); paper flowers
(Prima); decorative brads (Queen & Co.); ribbon (Making Memories); acrylic paint; stamping ink; buttons; bulletin board; cardstock

A little bit of paint allows you to alter the color of just about anything. While your paintbrush is still wet, paint the chipboard letters for a couple of other projects like this inspirational book and bulletin board.

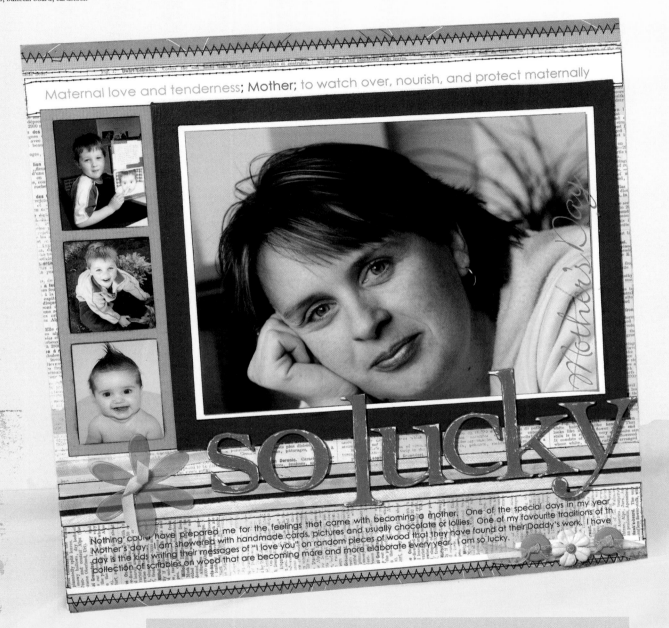

Maternal love and tenderness; **Mother;** to watch over, nourish, and protect maternally

so lucky

Nothing could have prepared me for the feelings that came with becoming a mother. One of the special days in my year Mother's day; I am showered with handmade cards, pictures and usually chocolate or lollies. One of my favourite traditions of th day is the kids writing their messages of "I love you" on random pieces of wood that they have found at their Daddy's work. I have collection of scribbles on wood that are becoming more and more elaborate every year. I am so lucky.

So Lucky

Combine a stunning self-portrait, three cutey-pie kids and a fabulous sense of color and design and you get Nic's happy Mother's Day tribute—to herself! Hand-cut, paint and sand chipboard letters to make a striking title. Add machine-stitching for a touch of homey texture. Use acrylic and paper flowers, along with ribbons and buttons, to add just the right amount of femininity to the layout.

Bulletin board

Paint frame of bulletin board with acrylic paint. Cut patterned-paper strips to form mitered frame for bulletin board. Mat paper frame on cardstock using a sewing machine to adhere. Ink all edges with black pen. Cut out chipboard letters and large photo corner elements; paint with acrylic paint, sand when dry and adhere to front of bulletin board. Tie ribbons around frame and embellish frame with additional ribbon, paper flowers and brads. To finish, glue buttons and acrylic flowers to plain thumbtacks to create decorative tacks.

Inspirational book

The base of this book is a cardstock file-folder shape. Cut doubled-tabbed, graduated pages to fold in half and fit inside file folder. Stack pages on unfolded cover; punch two evenly spaced holes in center and thread ribbon through to create tied binding. Decorate pages with sewn patterned paper, written sentiments, bits of ribbon, buttons, paper flowers and decorative brads. Ink all edges to add dimension. Adorn cover with cut-out, painted and sanded chipboard letters, ribbons, acrylic flower and sewn paper.

Milestone *Moment*

by Tricia

Teen boys and the men in your life will love having industrial elements on their layouts. Here wire mesh adds just the right amount of masculinity to the frame and card as well.

Supplies: Patterned papers (7 Gypsies, KI Memories, Li'l Davis Designs, Pebbles); stickers (7 Gypsies); letter stickers (Sticker Studio); charms, hinges (Making Memories); brads (Creative Impressions); ribbons (Li'l Davis Designs, Making Memories); rub-ons (My Mind's Eye); stamps (Inkadinkado, Postmodern Design); woven label (Me & My Big Ideas); metal-rimmed tag (Avery); wood frame (Michaels); wire mesh screen; stamping ink; picture hanger; denim; cardstock; envelope

Congratulations

Tricia's graduation page and remnant art pieces are urban, edgy and totally teen. Layer and mount hardware-inspired elements to make this page truly masculine. Add license-plate letter stickers to create the perfect title for a ultra-male finishing touch.

Decorated frame

Paint edges of wooden frame with black acrylic paint. Cover frame front with torn pieces of patterned-paper scraps from page. Tie ribbons around one side of frame. Glue metal embellishments on torn paper. Finish with a decorative monogram of bits of paper, mesh and a letter sticker.

Graduation card and envelope

Cut leftover wire mesh screen into rectangle and fold in half to create card base. Cover edges with ribbon remnants, both inside and out. Add decorative stitching to pieces of cardstock and adhere to card front. Affix letter stickers to create title. Attach key charm with wire to mesh. Tie ribbon around top of card and attach date-stamped tag. Create inside sentiment and attach behind front title. Decorate envelope with leftover ribbon and letter stickers.

Garden *Gaiety* *by Amy*

Outside, the garden is coming alive in spring. These charming seed packets carry that fresh feeling inside onto your layout as well as the pretty herb containers and tag book.

Supplies: Patterned paper, garden tags, labels (Melissa Frances); rub-on letters, shapes (KI Memories, Making Memories, Melissa Frances); chipboard letters (Heidi Swapp); ribbon slide, mini brads, letter embellishments (Junkitz); ribbon (Offray); index tab (Creative Imaginations); metal-rimmed tag (American Crafts); enameled herb containers (Heart & Home); loose-leaf ring; cardstock

Flowers are an obsession of mine. Big ones, little ones, short ones, & fat ones; I have never met a flower I didn't like. My special passion is perennials. Each year in March, I race to the gardens to remove last years mulch of leaves to discover the tender shoots trying to push their way through the soil and debris. This process of rebirth is food for my soul.

Amazing

MY

Garden *fever*

My Garden Fever

Soft shades of pastel green sing of spring, making the photos on Amy's fresh-as-a-daisy page pop while bringing a reminiscent feel to the remnant art on the next page. Crop and layer pale patterns and colors for the background to create an understated platform for close-up photos of delicate flowers. Choose dainty embellishments to add a subtle finish to the page.

More Than
28 a Page

Herb containers

Print, crop and adhere tags to fronts of containers. Embellish with leftover ribbon pieces and garden tags attached to ribbon with jump rings.

Wildflowers tag book

Print sentiments in circular text boxes onto leftover patterned paper. Cut printed paper into circle-shaped pages. Cut same-sized circles from chipboard. Adhere printed paper to front and back of each chipboard circle and adhere ribbon loop under patterned paper to create book pages. Punch hole in top of each page. Add additional page embellishments including envelopes, patterned paper with printed sentiments, seed packets and preprinted tags. Bind book together through holes with metal ring. Tie remaining ribbon scraps onto ring to finish.

Outdoor *Allure*

by Kathy

Texture and rub-on letters can provide a distressed feel that looks great on a layout about a little boy who loves to fish. This same feel can be a great addition to your cards and journals just right for gift giving.

Supplies: Patterned papers (Daisy D's, Karen Foster Design); rub-ons (My Mind's Eye); perforating cutting blade, stone letters (EK Success); mini hanger (Card Connection); gel paint, decoupage medium (Plaid); safety pins, brads (Making Memories); buckle (Junkitz); ribbon (Offray); papier-mâché pencil holder (Michaels); composition book; stamping ink; acrylic paint; transparency; craft sticks; cardstock; envelope

Fishing From the Dock

Kathy sets the rustic tone of her fishing layout by converting her photos to sepia. Roll an inked perforating cutting blade on the patterned-paper background to make meandering lines reminiscent of stitching as a page accent. Paint craft-stick title to echo the planks of the dock in the photos. Add bright green splashes across the layout to create a sense of playfulness.

Pencil holder

Cover a papier-mâché pencil holder by cutting a strip of patterned-paper remnant wider than holder and long enough to overlap. Adhere paper strip around outside of holder. Fold excess to inside and adhere. Adhere contrasting strip of patterned paper from page scraps on inside of holder. Apply decoupage medium to holder and let dry. Adhere ribbon scrap around top edge both inside and out to complete the holder.

Birthday card and envelope

Print "Happy" onto scrap patterned paper from page; cut to size and attach to card. Adhere contrasting strip of paper along bottom of card. Brush gel paint on edges of card and on lower right of card front. Apply leftover rub-on letters over gel paint. Adhere knotted ribbon to add finishing touch. Decorate envelope with patterned paper, rub-on letters and additional patterned paper as address block.

Decorated journal

Cover the front, back and spine of a composition book with remaining patterned papers and cardstock from page. Adhere snippets of ribbon to hide seams of paper. Add rub-on letters to create title. Outline rub-on letters with brown ink. Write random words on patterned paper. Brush gel paint on edges. Finish with premade letter elements.

Playtime Glee *by Nic*

Once you find the perfect, playful font for a springtime outing to the park, use it again to convey that same youthful spirit on a board book and birthday card.

Supplies: Patterned paper (Junkitz); letter stamps (PSX Design); ribbon (American Traditional Designs); decorative brads (Queen & Co.); felt marker (EK Success); board book; cardstock; gesso; sandpaper; envelope

This winter was long with the boys asking constantly if we could go to the park, but with Abby at crawling stage and the ground so wet and cold, we didn't often go. "Can we go to the park" was always met with a no... it was something that made me feel incredibly guilty, but on the other hand I knew it was a time-of-life thing. Abby wouldn't always be that small.

SPRING playtime

TOGETHER

FUN TIME

Finally we got some dry weather and Abby grew up enough to be less pesky! Paul & I surprised the kids one beautiful day by stopping at the park. The raised eyebrows, the smiles and the "Are we really going to play here?" was reward enough. The kids ran and played on the bars, slides and the tyre swing. We spent a good amount of time just relaxing at the park. It was nice to sit in the sun and feel good about seeing the kids play.

march 2005

Spring Playtime

Simple, graphic lines accentuate Nic's playful layout. Nic uses her son's surroundings to create a self-framing photo that draws the viewer's eye directly to the subject of the photo. Echo the curves in the focal photo by rounding the corners of the photos and mats and by using a circular element on the subtitle to create a sense of unity throughout the layout.

Altered board book

Sand front and back cover and all pages of board book. Apply gesso to all surfaces of book (one page at a time) and let dry. Cut cardstock and patterned-paper page remnants to create backgrounds for each page. Add machine-stitched elements to background and adhere to pages of book. Stamp sentiments onto background papers. Print journaling and cut into strips. Ink edges of journaling strips and adhere to backgrounds. Cover book with leftover cardstock and add sewn patterned-paper elements. Mount photos throughout book. Handcut title from cardstock and adhere to cover. Finish cover with stamped sentiment and ribbon ties.

Birthday card and envelope

Fold cardstock rectangle to create card base. Cut circle from patterned-paper scrap. Mat strips of contrasting remnant paper to cardstock, adhere circle over strips of paper and machine-stitch. Adhere to card. Add handcut paper letters, squares and strip to decorate card front. Randomly ink elements on card front. Finish sentiment with stamped words. For envelope, cut out middles from rectangles to create paper "rings." Ink edges of rectangles. Arrange and adhere to cardstock. Mat cardstock and glue to front of envelope. Add stamped sentiment.

With one package of metal embellishments you can create a whole array of different looks. Wipe a little acrylic paint on them for a softer look on a baby layout or leave them plain for a bolder statement on a card or door hanger.

Supplies: Patterned papers (Autumn Leaves); mailbox letters, photo corners, ribbon slides, flower charms (Making Memories); ribbon (Offray); wooden flowers (Li'l Davis Designs); frame (Michaels); game tiles; cardstock; lace; acrylic paint

Carly, I adore this picture! You were such a happy baby, and so pretty in pink. Having a girl is so much fun. I can't get enough of ribbons, lace, rosebuds and of course - pink!

ALL PINK

All Pink

Baby girls and pink are a match made in heaven. Tricia combines vintage-feel prints to create a timeless backdrop for a favorite photo. Add wooden accents and game tiles for dimension. Complete the feminine feel of this cheerful layout by adorning page with lace and gingham ribbon.

Tricia's tip:

Use lace scraps to create a lovely accent on your layout. Carry the accent over to paper crafts made with page leftovers for dainty, feminine charm.

Door hanger

Start with a square of leftover cardstock, adhere patterned-paper remnant strips to cardstock. Punch holes, evenly spaced, all around edge. Decorate hanger front with mailbox letters, metal accents and ribbon. Thread ribbon in sewing fashion through holes around hanger. Add knotted ribbon hanger to finish.

Decorated frame

Trace frame and opening onto backside of patterned paper left over from page. Cut out patterned paper along lines. Adhere to front of frame. Cut diamond shapes from patterned-paper scraps and adhere to lower right corner of frame. Adorn frame with lace and buckled ribbon. Add mailbox letter, painted metal flower, wooden flower and ribbon remnant to complete.

Baby card and envelope

Create card base from cardstock scrap. Tear strip off bottom of card front to expose inside of card underneath. Cover card with slightly smaller piece of scrap patterned paper torn along bottom edge. Adorn card front with additional strips of contrasting patterned-paper scraps and leftover game tiles, mailbox letters, ribbon and metal ribbon slides. Adhere strip of patterned paper along bottom edge of inside of card so that it shows beyond torn edge of card front. Create matching envelope and embellish with metal elements and ribbon from the remainder of the page scraps.

Wedded *Bliss*

by Courtney

When you combine a variety of complementary papers in your layout, you open the door to a whole host of paper-crafting looks. Concentrate on the blue papers for a cool-toned gift bag or altered CD; play up the red papers for a romantic wedding card.

Supplies: Patterned papers (Autumn Leaves, Chatterbox); stitched tag, letter stickers (Chatterbox); rub-on elements (Basic Grey); buttons (Junkitz); ribbon (Offray); gel pen; cardstock; CD; gift bag; tissue paper

A Perfect Match

Courtney turns up the "wow" factor with her unique wedding page. Start with a black background and silver accents to lend elegance to the layout. Crop and round the corners of patterned papers with bold patterns and bright colors to create a sassy background for a formal black-and-white photo to create a sense of energy. Add title and journaling in white so that elements pop from the page.

Gift bag and tag

Cover bottom section of bag with patterned paper left over from creating page, hiding seams of paper in folds. Adhere contrasting patterned paper remnants to upper portion of bag. Add ribbon scraps around top of bag. Replace existing handles with knotted ribbon handles to coordinate. Create tag by folding cardstock scrap rectangle in half. Adhere strips of contrasting patterned paper remnants to tag and adorn with button, ribbon and rub-on sentiment. Stuff with colored tissue paper for an elegant finish.

Altered CD

Trace CD onto backside of patterned paper scrap and cut circle. Adhere to CD front. Cut strips of contrasting paper remnants and adhere. Apply leftover letter stickers to create sentiment and add handwritten subtitle. Add a photo and button to front of CD. Lightly ink edges of CD to complete.

Wedding card and envelope

Fold wide strip of cardstock scrap in half to create card base. Punch two holes through card base on left side. Thread ribbon remnant through holes. Adhere patterned-paper scraps to card front. Cut two circles from black cardstock to create tags. Punch holes in tags. Machine-stitch around edge of tag and hole. Tie tags with ribbon snippets. Adhere one tag to card front. Decorate tags and card front with leftover rub-ons. Make coordinating envelope from patterned-paper scraps. Adhere remaining tag to envelope. Apply letter stickers to envelope for sentiment.

Time *Passage*

by Courtney

Don't throw away any scrap of paper. When you do something like cover chipboard letters with patterned paper you'll have plenty of leftovers to create fun card embellishments, clipboard backgrounds and gift box sets.

Supplies: Patterned papers (Chatterbox); chipboard letters, rub-on words, tag, epoxy letter (Making Memories); buttons (Junkitz); decoupage medium (Plaid); ribbon; embroidery floss; stamping ink; silk flower; cardstock; clipboard; box; acrylic paint

remember

together

a busy

ANNIVERSARY

December 10 2004

Ok, I admit it... sometimes it's difficult sharing my husband with an audience of 800 on our anniversary. You'd think after 5 yrs. I'd be used to it—this is, after all, our job, but still... the dream of the candlelit dinner, the roses, the jewels... well, that is overshadowed by the quest for proper lighting, smooth set changes & a spotlight operator who will stay awake. Yep. We're in the theatre. It's what we do, and since we do it at a church, we always do it at Christmas. 5 years together & some things never change. Oddly, I'm okay with this. We thrive on it. We wrote this show, directed it. Adam was in it... and a lot of amazing people celebrated 'us' with us. Yep. This is it. Our 5 year anniversary... glowing, shining & the most in love we've ever been. 2004

A Busy Anniversary

Courtney shares the frenetic story of her not-so-private anniversary, mimicked in the busy and chaotic patterns on her page title. Turn all the photos black-and-white and reduce the support photos to allow you sufficient room to include a large number of photos without overwhelming the page. Add handwritten journaling for a personal touch.

Embellished clipboard

Adhere collaged bits of torn patterned-paper scraps to cover clipboard. Coat with decoupage medium and let dry. Paint clip and let dry. Glue chipboard letters to lower left of clipboard. Glue silk flower with epoxy letter center to front of clip. Tie with ribbon to complete.

Monogram gift box and tag

Cover box with patterned-paper remnants from page and cut out diamond shapes. Cover leftover chipboard letter with cardstock, ink and apply to box front. Cover top of box with solid paper scrap, adding thin strip around edge of box top. Tie box with ribbon. Cut tag shape from cardstock scrap and adhere torn strips of ribbon to tag. Add cutout pattern elements from scrap paper. Staple cardstock "to" and "from" label onto front. Tie with ribbon.

Love card and envelope

Create card base from folded cardstock scrap. Cut title from patterned paper remnants and adhere to card. Cut cardstock hearts and lightly ink edges. Adhere hearts to upper right of card front and adorn with buttons. Write sentiments around card elements. Ink edges of card to complete. Make matching envelope from patterned paper. Adorn with pieces of remaining patterned paper, cardstock hearts and buttons. Ink edges of envelope to finish.

To Do
- get groceries
- Run to Bank
- Pay Bills
- Finish Newsletter
- Plan Menu
- Laundry!!
- Write up announcements
- Call people for fundraiser

- Pick up food for a.m. meeting
- Send photos to Carrie
- B'Day gift for Dad
- Run to

SUMMER

Summer is filled with warm breezes, glowing sunsets and scents of blossoms in full bloom. We take summer vacations, celebrate holidays with picnics and barbecues, play on sandy beaches and relax to renew our minds and bodies. This season gives us cause to take long and lingering walks, visit local zoos and celebrate our fathers and forefathers. We seek out the freshness of cool swimming pools, lakes and streams. Summer brings a plethora of reasons to scrapbook our most treasured memories. Reflect on the ideas in this chapter to inspire your own summer layouts and paper crafts.

When my friend showed me this photo of a beach in Thailand he visited recently, I was struck by how my senses reacted. I can still feel those reactions each time I study this photo. I immediately feel relaxed, sun-kissed and cuddled by the warmth of the sunshine. I can smell the salt water and sea breeze that blows through the palm trees. It makes me think of summer – and although it is cold and wet here today, I can feel the promise of summers to come. I can feel relaxed and renewed just by looking at this serene scene and enjoying the peaceful ambiance of a sandy beach in the summer.

Dad's *Devotion*

by Tricia

Three-dimensional accents like keys, bottle caps and watch faces really make your layouts pop. And because they usually are sold in packs, you'll find the 3-D fun is easy to mix into your cards and home décor, too.

Supplies: Patterned papers (Rusty Pickle); stickers (7 Gypsies, EK Success, Me & My Big Ideas, Rusty Pickle); key (K & Company); bottle caps (Design Originals); watch face, ribbon (Li'l Davis Designs); heart charm (Darice); walnut ink (Ranger); brads (Creative Impressions); label holder, photo corners (Making Memories); woven label (Me & My Big Ideas); papier-mâché letter (Michaels); cardstock

Celebrating Dad

As a "queen of collage," Tricia deftly combines patterns, textures, colors and interesting objects to create this love-worn tribute to a special dad. Collage patterned papers for background; machine-stitch to add a casual yet subtle finish. Lightly sand the edges of the page elements to complete the timeless feel.

Altered monogram

Cut several long strips of patterned-paper scraps to match the depth of the letter. Adhere strips around entire edge of letter. Trace letter onto back of patterned paper. Cut out along guidelines and adhere to letter front. Gently sand edges of letter. Apply stickers to bottle caps and glue to front of letter. Adorn letter front with ribbon remnants and leftover labels, charms and stickers to complete.

Father's Day card and envelope

Make card base from folded cardstock. Collage patterned-paper scraps to create card background, adding machine-stitching as desired. Adhere sanded sentiment strips to card front. Apply stickers to cardstock and run through printer to print title; punch into tag shape, add stapled ribbon and adhere to card. Adorn card with charms to finish. Create coordinating envelope from remnant of patterned paper. Decorate envelope with strips of contrasting patterned paper and randomly placed leftover stickers.

Father *Love* *by Nic*

Denim—you love to wear it, but did you know you can scrap with it as well? You can get a multitude of effects from this versatile fabric—from the crisp new look on a layout and gift bag to the frayed, comfortable feel on a notebook and bookmark.

Supplies: Patterned papers (Basic Grey); decorative brads (Queen & Co.); letter stickers (Chatterbox); rub-on words, chipboard letters (Making Memories); decoupage medium, paper paint (Plaid); solvent ink (Tsukineko); notebook (ACCO); denim; cardstock; rickrack

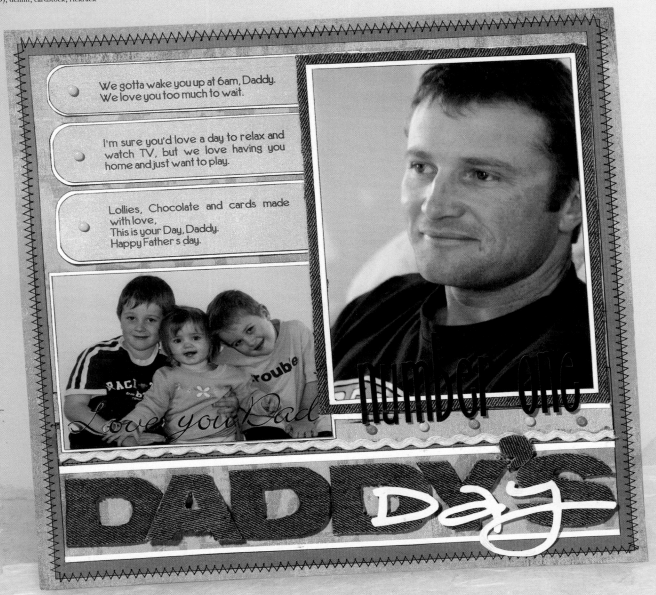

Daddy's Day

Muted, rich colors match the sentiment of Nic's Father's Day creation. Crop, layer and stitch background papers. Use denim to add a touch of masculinity to the layout. Journal from a child's perspective to add a playful and heartfelt touch.

Nic's tip:

If you run out of the more commonly used letters when using alphabet rub-ons, you can adapt the others. For example, a "d" can become an "a." Just use scissors and your imagination!

Coordinating gift bag and tag

Cover gift bag with patterned-paper remnants. Mat strips of patterned paper and embellish with machine-stitching, strips of denim and rickrack. Miter-cut patterned paper frame; insert photo behind and double mat on cardstock. Adhere framed photo on bag front. Finish with leftover rub-on sentiment and stripped denim handles. Create tag out of matted cardstock and handcut letters. Decorate tag with remaining brads and pieces of denim.

Coordinating notebook and bookmark

Remove and discard spiral binding from notebook. Cover front and back covers with patterned paper scraps. Adhere contrasting strip of patterned paper. Cut out rounded rectangular "rings" of patterned paper and lightly ink edges. Adhere paper rings to cover. Handcut title letters and coat with clear lacquer; adhere to cover. Using existing holes in cover, set four eyelets in front and back cover. Join covers and pages of notebook together using loose-leaf rings through eyelets. Tie strips of denim scraps to rings to finish.

For bookmark, cut rectangle from patterned-paper scraps and round two of the corners. Decorate with machine-stitching, brads, patterned paper strips, handcut letters and remaining rub-ons. Mat rectangle with cardstock and ink edges. Finish bookmark with denim strip tied through eyelet.

Outdoor *Play*

by Shannon

One simple roll of paper mesh can breathe new life in your layouts. Use it as a subtle background texture, as in the layout and album, or showcase it as a bold design element, like on the notepad and holder.

Supplies: Patterned papers, mini brads (Junkitz); ribbon (American Crafts); rub-on letters (Making Memories); wooden letters (Li'l Davis Designs); mesh (Magic Mesh); pen

SPLASH

2004

The child, he splashes in the water because the day could get no hotter. Cool & crisp, the creek does feel as droplets hit his face with zeal. But cautious as ever for fear of never wanting to fall in, the boy remains in shallow spots and starts to splash again.

Robby - 2005

Splash

Shannon's energetic layout is as all-American as it is all-boy! Combine hot red and cool blue patterned papers to convey the feeling of the hot summer sun and the cool splash of water. Add texture and interest with patterned ribbon, mesh and brads. Finish the layout with a fun poem to serve as journaling.

Shannon's tip:

Save interesting packaging. You can use empty
scrapbooking supply boxes for the base of a note holder or gift box.

Tag mini album

Begin by cutting five identical tags from cardstock. Cover both sides of each
tag with leftover cardstock or patterned paper. Punch six evenly spaced holes
along the edge of each tag. Embellish each tag with handwritten sentiments,
photos, pieces of ribbon, bits of patterned paper and wooden numbers. Fold
patterned-paper strips in half and secure with brad to end of each tag. Tie tags
together with ribbon remnants through punched holes to bind book.

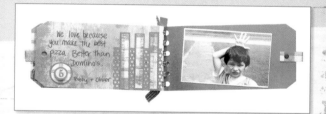

Embellished note holder

To make this cute and functional note holder, start by cutting down an empty
box to desired size and shape. Cover box with patterned-paper scraps. Embellish with remaining ribbon, decorative mesh, brads and wooden letters. Cut
sheets of blank notepaper to fit inside of the box to complete.

Home *Life*

by Torrey

Once you start cutting flower elements from your patterned paper, it can be hard to stop. And you may not want to, once you discover all the different ways to use them. Slightly curl the petals for an accent on photo cubes, or use pieces of them to trim cards, layouts and bulletin boards.

Supplies: Patterned papers (Amscan, Scenic Route Paper Co.); corrugated paper (Paper Company); fiber (EK Success); die-cut letters (QuicKutz); wooden numbers (Michaels); wooden beads (Darice); heart beads (Crafts Etc.); bulletin board, papier-mâché boxes (Hobby Lobby); brads; thumbtacks; cardstock; blank card and envelope; stamping ink

Although this is our first house; it's much more than just a house. It's our first home. I can't tell you how comforting it feels to know that these four walls and roof are actually ours. But what is it that makes this house a home? It's the sense of family that greets us at the door ...the love that paints these four walls ...the respect and acceptance that dwells and grows under this roof ...and it's the cat. Yep, 5270 is more than an address. It's home.

5270 Home

Torrey unifies her layout by manipulating her background photo and focal photo in an image-editing program. Mat photos with strips of patterned paper, mount on corrugated paper background. Accent edges with shapes cut from patterned paper. Add depth and texture to the layout with three-dimensional wooden elements.

Decorated bulletin board

Cover frame of bulletin board with strips of patterned paper left over from page. Adhere contrasting patterned paper over top portion of bulletin board and affix die-cut letters over patterned paper. Adorn corners of bulletin board with cutout paper elements. To complete, glue extra decorative beads onto thumbtacks.

Embellished photo cubes

Cover each side of the papier-mâché boxes with patterned paper remnants, using both sides of double-sided patterned paper. Ink all edges of the boxes. Decorate all sides of boxes using remaining beads, cutout paper elements and photos.

Thank-you card and envelope

Cover card front with patterned paper scraps. Add contrasting strips of patterned paper and cutout paper elements to card front and secure with brads. Adhere die-cut letters to card. Lightly ink edges of card to finish. For envelope, ink edges of envelope and add cardstock strip and cutout paper element to envelope front.

Water *Play* by Amy

A summery water-filled layout can be the springboard to amazing paper crafts. The funky color combination adds a fresh, playful touch to whatever you make, whether a board book or celebratory greeting card. Dive right in!

Supplies: Patterned papers, die-cut accents (My Mind's Eye); beads (Junkitz); conchos (Scrapworks); ribbon (KI Memories); rub-on letters (Heidi Swapp); word stickers (Creative Imaginations); card (Déjà Views); brads; children's board book

cool

water

sun

splash

splish splash

O the joy of my spirit— to splash the water! *Walt Whitman*

This was a year of firsts for you. First year at the beach without big sis, first year you had a boogie board and the first year you were able to go into the water without Mom & Dad having to hold you every moment. In fact, you were so completely unafraid of any aspect of the water. We were so proud that you have finally found your Sea Legs.

Splish Splash

Amy crafts this graphic, fun-in-the-sun layout from cool shades of coordinating tropical-colored patterned papers. Change photo to black-and-white to ensure it will not clash with the bright background. Add brads, ribbons and curved and linear accents to create a watery feeling on an oceangoing page.

Altered board book

Prepare the pages of the book by sanding them vigorously to remove shiny finish. With a damp cloth, wipe off any excess residue before adhering patterned-paper remnants to the front and back of each page. Embellish the pages with die cuts, quotes, sayings and photos. To complete the book, create a cover by adhering patterned paper and printed title to front.

Greeting card and envelope

Decorate a premade card with leftover square and rectangle blocks and small punched circles of patterned-paper scraps. Add word stickers and a ribbon bow to complete. Make a beautiful coordinating envelope created from patterned-paper remnants to perfectly match the card.

Amy's tip:

Create your own custom page elements such as quotes, titles and word borders using your computer to print on cardstock, photo paper and patterned-paper scraps.

Decorative bookmark

To create the bookmark, machine-stitch a scrap of patterned paper to a slightly larger contrasting piece using a zigzag stitch. Punch out coordinating circles of patterned paper and embellish each with its own rub-on letter. Tie with leftover ribbon to complete.

Beach *Fun*

by Kathy

The fun from a summertime layout is contagious! Splash that energy into your brag book, cards or anything else that could use a good dose of summer fun.

Supplies: Patterned papers (Kangaroo & Joey, Karen Foster Design, Provo Craft); gel slides, beach stickers, mini brads (Karen Foster Design); acrylic charms (Go West Studios); wooden letters, leather border (Li'l Davis Designs); letter stickers (American Crafts); traffic stickers (Moonshine Design); rub-ons (Making Memories); tabs (Creek Bank Creations); mini brads, safety pins (Queen & Co.); photo corners (3L); label maker (Dymo); ribbon (Offray); frame hangers (Bulldog); acrylic paint; stamping ink; primer; cardstock; blank card and envelope; paper bags

Skim Board Fun

Warm, sunny colors re-create the feeling of summer heat on Kathy's page. Distress a patterned paper background with paint and sanding. Create label-tape journaling and randomly adhere little elements to add terrific detail.

Paper bag brag book

Begin by stacking two paper bags together and folding them in half to create book. Staple bags along fold to secure together. Cover pages of book with patterned paper remnants, trim, stickers, ribbon, brads, handmade tags and photos as desired. Make a front and back cover for the book using patterned-paper scraps. Fold a cardstock strip to cover the spine. Punch three holes along spine and tie with ribbons. Adorn cover as desired with additional stickers, letters and charms.

Kathy's tip:

If wooden alphabets or accents are not the color you need for your project, use paint or ink to change the color. This allows you to use them for multiple projects.

Greeting card and envelope

Mat scrap patterned paper with cardstock and tie with ribbon. Add safety pin to ribbon and adhere to card. Affix leftover wooden letters and letter stickers to card, inking edges to complete. For envelope, ink edges of strips of patterned paper and adhere along top and bottom. Add remaining stickers and ink edges of envelope as finishing touch.

Patriotic *Pride*

by Shannon

When you find a great bargain on an unusual embellishment, like these felt stars, don't hesitate to take the plunge. Not only will they be a great addition to your layout, you can easily use them to jazz up home-décor projects or greeting cards.

Supplies: Patterned paper (Junkitz); ribbons (Making Memories, Offray); alpha ribbon charms (Making Memories); chipboard elements (Rusty Pickle); felt stars (Don Mechanic Enterprises); rickrack (Wrights); magnet set, wine box (Michaels); decoupage medium (Plaid); wire; acrylic paint; cardstock

here's baby elijah (as oliver always calls him) celebrating his very first fourth of july! we took tons of photos of him but my favorites are the ones seen here, especially the one of him sitting in the grass. the little guy looks like a baby gorilla with those sweet little arm & leg fat rolls. i just want to squeeze him.

American Baby

Shannon creates this star-studded layout to showcase a baby's first Independence Day. Stitch a layered background. Place ribbons horizontally across page. Use felt starts to effectively frame a focal photo. Place supporting photos to lead the viewer's eye in a cascade down the layout to end at the journaling.

Wine container

Machine-stitch strips of patterned-paper
scraps. Adhere sewn strips side by side
around wine container and lid. Use additional sewn strip of paper to conceal seam in
back. Coat lid and container with decoupage
medium. Add horizontal pieces of remaining
rickrack, felt star and ribbon as embellishment. Create ring out of several turns of
wire. Thread metal letters onto wire and tie
ribbon on wire ring. Finish container by adding wire ring to handle.

Greeting card and envelope

Create a card base from scrap cardstock. Embellish card front with
patterned paper, ribbon, painted chipboard piece and felt-star leftovers.
Make coordinating envelope out of additional patterned paper. Adorn
envelope with chipboard, ribbon and sewn cardstock circles. Finish
envelope with metal letters and felt star.

Magnets

Paint premade magnets with several coats of
white acrylic paint and let dry. Using page
leftovers, cover fronts of magnets with ribbon,
patterned paper, metal letters, felt stars and
photos as desired.

Proud *Patriot*

by Courtney

Patterned papers can have a chameleon-like quality depending on the cardstock colors you mix with them. The geometric papers used to make a patriotic layout take on a completely different look when combined with the summer green background, like in the mini album.

Supplies: Patterned papers, photo corners, stickers (Chatterbox); chipboard stars (Heidi Swapp); chipboard word (Li'l Davis Designs); rub-on letters (Creative Imaginations); acrylic paint; envelope; CD tin

happy

May the importance of freedom never escape you. May Independence Day be less about events and more about America. May you grow to cherish this country we are blessed to live in. May the love and pride of being an American rest on your shoulders. May you always be proud to call yourself an American... this is my 4th of July wish for you.

all★american

July 4th

Courtney puts a subtle twist on the classic red, white and blue by adding touches of green and yellow to her patriotic layout. Use floral paper to create the illusion of fireworks in a handcut patterned-paper title. Mount strong diagonal elements on the page for eye-catching visual interest.

Altered CD case and mini album

Create the base for a mini accordion-style book out of four card bases. Adhere front of one card to back of another in accordion fashion. Embellish pages with pieces of patterned paper scraps, chipboard stars, photos and hand-journaling. Gently sand all edges of book. Decorate cover of book with patterned paper, rub-ons and photo. Paint entire tin with acrylic paint. When dry, cover lid of tin with patterned paper left over from page. Decorate with chipboard letter, paper elements and rub-on letters.

Courtney's tip:

Find a new use for photo corners. Use them to create cheap and fun mats or borders.

Birthday card and envelope

Fold patterned-paper leftovers to create card base. Adhere contrasting strips of patterned paper diagonally across card front. Cut abstract candles and flames from patterned-paper pieces and glue to card. Add preprinted sentiment and one thin strip of patterned paper horizontally to card to finish. For envelope, cover with patterned paper. Adhere rounded rectangle and horizontal strip of contrasting papers across bottom of envelope. Add preprinted and handwritten sentiments to complete.

Beach *Bright*

by Amy

With your circle cutter close at hand for this bright and sunny summer layout, keep on cutting for other paper crafts. Make smaller circles out of patterned paper to adorn metal-rimmed accents to decorate a cute frame, playful greeting card or travel journal.

Supplies: Patterned papers, epoxy embellishments, coaster, metal-rimmed tags, stickers (Provo Craft); cotton tape (Imagination Project); ribbon (Offray); acrylic letters (KI Memories); brads; cardstock; wooden journal cover; wooden picture frame

wonderful summer

sand

&

sun

Smile

Our family has an annual tradition of traveling to the Cape each year for a vacation. Our parent started this tradition on thier honeymoon and we have been going back ever since that time. Sophie was introduced to this wonderful vacation spot in her very first year of life and absolutely trembles with delight at the prospect of retuning each year.

Sand & Sun

Nothing says "vacation" like a trip to the beach. Amy's use of bright citrus colors infuses her layout with that island feel. Crop circular patterned-paper shapes and one photo to accentuate the photos without overwhelming them. Layer epoxy embellishments, acrylic letter and ribbons to add visual appeal to the layout.

Decorated frame

Cover a premade wooden frame with patterned-paper scraps in an offset grid. Hide the paper seams with remnants of ribbon. Add decorative tags and acrylic letters to customize your frame. Gently sand the edges of the paper after it's been adhered for a soft finish.

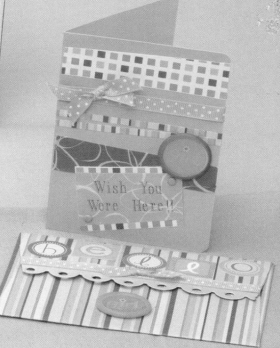

Greeting card and envelope

Create a card base from folded paper. Adorn front of card with odd-shaped strips of patterned paper, ribbon, sentiment tags and epoxy embellishments left over from the page. Create envelope out of remaining patterned paper, epoxy elements and letter stickers to perfectly match the card.

Travel journal

Cover both sides of the cover of an unfinished wood journal. Embellish with epoxy elements and coordinating patterned-paper strips. Decorate coaster element using die cuts, epoxy embellishment and printed title. Adhere to front of journal. Cut cardstock scraps to create page inserts. Punch holes in pages and attach rings through covers and all pages. Tie ribbon remnants to rings to decorate. Thread remaining ribbon through holes in front and back covers to create book tie to complete.

Travel *Texture*

by Torrey

Finding the perfect ribbon to match your patterned paper can sometimes be a challenge, but once you've found it—use it! Wrap it around a card or use just a snippet to adorn a handle on a cute purse. A little or a lot—ribbon rocks!

Supplies: Patterned papers (Magenta); ribbon (Michaels); wooden cigar box, purse handle, hardware (Darice); clock works (Walnut Hollow); envelope; clear lacquer; transparency film; empty ribbon spool; chalk; cardstocks

MEXICO

This was my first cruise! I went with the girls from Spellbinders. It was a quick 3-day jaunt to Ensenada, Mexico from L.A. We spent most of the time teaching scrapbooking onboard the ship. But when we got to Mexico, we just had to get off and see what we could in a day. We found a cheap bus tour then we went shopping for souvenirs in the flea market. This man was at La Bufadora (the blowhole) in traditional Aztec regalia doing a ceremonial dance... for a price.

2005

Mexico

The vibrant, playful colors Torrey chose for her layout scream, "Viva el scrapbooking!" Her placement of the red hibiscus photo draws the viewer's eye across the page to rest at the journaling. Use the negative space left from a handcut title rather than using the letters themselves. Finish off the page by adding just a touch of clear lacquer to give added dimension.

Wooden purse

Carefully remove and set aside all hardware from wooden purse. Cover the lid with patterned paper remnants from page, using a strip of coordinating paper to wrap around the edges. Cover the body of the purse in the same fashion, adding strips of patterned paper along the top and bottom edges for decoration. Reattach all hardware. Tie ribbon scraps to the left side of the handle for the final embellishment.

Ribbon spool clock

Start by covering an empty ribbon spool with patterned paper and cardstock scraps. Punch a hole in the middle of the back and front of the spool and feed the clockworks through the hole. Assemble the clockworks according to the manufacturer's directions. To finish the clock, use bits of leftover ribbon that is wound around the spool and tied in a bow at the top.

Greeting card and envelope

Make the card base out of folded cardstock. Cover the front with two coordinating patterned papers and adhere a tied ribbon to hide the seam. Use clear lacquer to highlight elements in the paper's pattern. Add a handwritten sentiment. To decorate the envelope, adhere a strip of remaining patterned paper down the side to complete.

Zootiful *Day*

by Amy

Supplies: Patterned papers, rub-on letters, accents (Imagination Project); metal letters (American Crafts); chipboard circles (Bazzill); ribbon (Offray); cardstock; CD

When versatile embellishments like these metal letters come with multiple colors in a pack, take advantage of the opportunity to let loose. Mix the colors for words in your headline on the layout, or to personalize gifts for loved ones.

Wildlife in the Bronx Zoo

Mosaic-blocked photos and patterned paper come together to create Amy's graphic layout reminiscent of a magazine advertisement. Place journaling vertically along page edge to keep the focus on the photos while adding that all-important story to explain them. Offset the linear look with patterned paper-covered chipboard circles.

Amy's tip:

Keep your photos as the center of your layouts by enlarging great shots and keeping the embellishments simple and to a minimum.

Altered CD and case

Burn a CD with favorite music. Cover CD with patterned paper remnants, cutting hole out of center. Decorate with bits of ribbon and rub-on sentiments. Cover premade tag board CD holder with patterned-paper scraps. Add rub-ons and metal letters to create title.

Birthday card and envelope

Create card base from folded patterned-paper scraps. Punch patterned-paper circles for balloons. Add strips of contrasting paper for balloon strings. Assemble and adhere balloons to card. Use leftover rub-on letters to add sentiment. Glue ribbon over balloon strings to finish. Make a coordinating envelope from patterned-paper remnants adorned with strips of contrasting paper and sentiment created from rub-on letters.

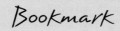

Bookmark

Cut a tag shape from patterned-paper scraps. Mat with contrasting patterned paper. Add paper strips in zigzag pattern on tag. Use remaining rub-on letters to create sentiment. Affix leftover metal letters to front. Punch hole in top of tag and tie with ribbon to complete.

Backyard *Bliss* by Nic

So, you've got this package of great letters, but your supply of them is dwindling. Don't be afraid to mix and combine upper- and lowercase letters to create a great title on your layout or use them individually for monograms on cards and gifts.

Supplies: Patterned papers (Heidi Swapp, Scenic Route Paper Co.); chipboard letters (www.everlastingkeep-sakes.com); rub-on letters (Déjà Views); painted twill (Autumn Leaves); circle charms, epoxy letters, bookplate (Li'l Davis Designs); word stickers (Destination Scrapbook Designs); ribbon (Doodlebug Design); cardstock; acrylic paint; chipboard; papier-mâché box

Barbecue

You can almost smell that wonderful barbecue aroma and hear that telltale sizzle, thanks to Nic's mouth-watering focal photo. Use an oversized title to balance the photo placement, running clever journaling strips above and below the title. Use vibrant, split-complementary colors to create a sense of energy on borders and beneath journaling.

Recipe box

Paint papier-mâché box with white acrylic paint. Cut pieces of patterned paper remnants slightly smaller than each side of box and each face of lid. Ink edges of patterned-paper pieces and adhere to box and lid. Glue leftover ribbon around bottom edge of box. Cut frames from chipboard and paint with acrylic paint. Cover frames with inked patterned paper. Adhere contrasting patterned paper to back of frame. Glue frames to each side of box. Cover lid with matted patterned-paper scraps. Add bookplate with painted twill threaded through. Complete box lid with contrasting patterned-paper circles, chipboard letters, rub-ons and letter charms. Fill box with custom-made recipe cards and tabbed dividers made from cardstock and patterned paper. Add category labels with printed paper.

Nic's tip:

Use a patterned paper that has an overall repetitive pattern. This way you can use scraps of it that will join together very easily.

Thank-you card and envelope

Make card base out of folded cardstock. Collage patterned-paper scraps and cardstock pieces on card front and adorn with machine-stitching. Embellish with ribbon and brads. Decorate with leftover rub-ons, word sticker and chipboard letter. Create a matching envelope from remaining patterned paper decorated in similar fashion. Add printed journaling strip to envelope front and finish with epoxy letters.

Reunion *Rhapsody*

by Jodi

Supplies: Patterned papers, acrylic letters, printed transparency, die-cut accents, rub-on accents (KI Memories); ribbon (Michaels); coasters (Bazzill); envelope (DieCuts with a View); notebook (Hot Off The Press); decoupage medium (Plaid); stamping ink; cardstock

Transparencies, like these swirly flowers, can come in a full sheet, but you don't need to use them all in one place. Sprinkle a few on your layout—even the partial ones—then you'll have plenty of leftovers to decorate fu projects such as coasters and mini binders.

family

Jodi captures treasured moments of her family reunion in her warm and inviting layout. Encircle the focal photo with small supporting photos to create a comfortable sense of togetherness. Use welcoming, earthy colors and cutout transparency elements to enhance the outdoor theme.

Mini binder

Cover binder with matted patterned paper from page remnants. Ink edges and binding with brown ink. Cut out leftover transparency elements and adhere to front of binder. Tie ribbon scrap around binder cover. Create tabbed dividers from cardstock. Punch holes into dividers and place in binder. Fill with lined paper.

Greeting card and envelope

Fold cardstock to create card base. Adhere patterned-paper strips along edge of card. Punch squares along bottom of card. Frame punched windows with contrasting patterned-paper scraps. Adhere transparency behind windows. Cut rings from patterned paper and adhere randomly to card with acrylic letters and number. Add rub-ons and ribbon to finish. For envelope, adhere strip of remaining patterned paper to envelope. Add rub-on elements to decorate.

Coasters

Trace coasters onto cardstock and cut out. Adhere cardstock to coasters. Ink edges and apply die cuts randomly. Glue remaining printed transparency cutouts to top of coasters. Paint each coaster with decoupage medium, applying several times to coat. Dry thoroughly.

FALL

Fall is vibrant with the colors of autumn—the season of changes. Crisp, cool air envelops us as we take long walks, crunching fallen leaves with each step. Kids reluctantly find themselves back in school, county fairs abound, harvest vegetables grace our dinner tables and haunting ghouls seek out treasures of sweets and treats. We spend time counting our blessings and celebrating our grandparents. As you flip through the following chapter, let these layouts be inspiration for your own pages and art dedicated to all that comes with fall.

Autumn *Splendor*

by Torrey

By using hints of black, you can enhance the colors in your photos and patterned papers, making them even more vibrant. Don't be afraid to carry those same color choices into your home décor and decorative paper crafts as well.

Supplies: Patterned papers (Basic Grey, Scenic Route Paper Co.); flower punch (Family Treasures); heart punch (Emagination Crafts); ribbon, wreath (Hobby Lobby); composition book; vellum; stamping ink; cardstock; clear lacquer; card base and envelope; hot glue

Aspenglow

Torrey makes certain her stunning photo takes center stage on her layout. Make meticulous color choices of the patterned papers to help the photo literally jump off the page. Handcut a title and add interesting journaling for all the embellishment this striking layout needs.

More Than
70 a Page

Embellished wreath

Punch flowers and handcut leaves from contrasting patterned-paper remnants. Glue punched flowers together and bend slightly into cupped shape. Wrap wreath with remaining ribbon and tie decorative bow. Hot glue flowers and leaves onto wreath. Handcut sentiment from patterned paper; mat with cardstock and sand edges of letters. Glue sentiment to top of wreath. Brush clear lacquer onto flowers and leaves to finish.

Sympathy card and envelope

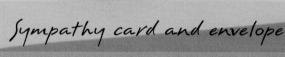

Arrange rectangles of patterned-paper scraps from page onto card. Punch heart out of patterned paper and double mat with black cardstock and contrasting patterned paper. Attach graduated curved strips of cardstock to back of heart and affix to card front. Punch hearts out of leftover vellum and place on card. Ink all edges of card to complete. Make envelope by adhering cardstock strip and adhere double-matted punched heart and shadow vellum heart to envelope.

Decorated journal

Cover front and back of composition book with patterned paper remnants from page. Adhere multiple strips of contrasting paper and cardstock along black binding edge. Handcut letters from patterned paper and adhere to rounded cardstock rectangle. Add decorative corners to title block and adhere. Complete by adding cardstock corners to journal.

Harvest *Time*

Take a cue from your patterned paper to create organic shapes in your layout—just follow the dotted line! Then incorporate those same freewheeling shapes in your brag book or artist trading card.

Supplies: Patterned papers (KI Memories); letter stickers (Arctic Frog); buckle (Junkitz); ribbon (May Arts, Michaels); rub-on letters and numbers (Li'l Davis Designs); pin back (Darice); Velcro; stamping ink; cardstock

Oh how I love fall!

Last year, we discovered Edwards' Apple Orchard... at the very end of the season.

This year, as soon as the slightest hint of fall arrived,

we made our first trip out there, and we had a blast!

There were tractors, trains, pumpkins, a petting zoo... and of course, those sinful apple donuts!

What a fun day! Yep. I love fall... and from the looks of it... so do you!

septeMber '05

fall fun

Bright, energetic colors and bold design elements come together to create Courtney's unique tribute to fall activities. Combine the traditional autumn colors of brown, orange and golden yellow with tropical aqua and lime green to make the layout fun, vivacious and playful. Adhere letter-sticker title and journaling strips to draw eye down and across the page. Showcase supporting photos in an embellished, filmstrip style.

Courtney's tip:

Utilize the patterns on paper to their full advantage
by cutting them apart at different places in their design
to create a multitude of looks from the same paper.

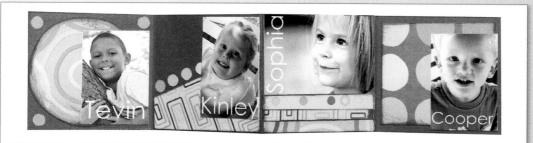

Mini brag-book pin

Start by cutting two strips of cardstock in contrasting colors. Accordion-fold strips to create five sections. Glue folded strips back to back to create base for book. Adorn each page of book with patterned paper remnants and photos. To create closure for book, glue strip of cardstock centered across back of book so that ends of strip protrude beyond book. Affix Velcro to top side of one end of strip and bottom side of opposite end of strip to create closure. Collapse book and wrap strip around book so that Velcro holds strip in place. Write title on front of strip. Glue pin closure to back of book to complete.

Artist trading card

Cut cardstock to size and ink edges. Adhere contrasting piece of leftover patterned paper slightly askew over card base. Decorate card front with additional strips of patterned-paper scraps, bits of ribbon and photo. Personalize card by writing a sentiment or name on strips of cardstock and adhere to card front. Punch hole in upper right corner of card and tie with ribbon.

Fall *Adventures*

by Torrey

Once you learn a cool new technique, like curling the edges of stitched paper, you won't want to quit. Keep going—use the same technique to accent tags, cards or any of your paper crafts.

Supplies: Patterned papers (Creative Imaginations, Rusty Pickle); ribbon (Michaels); photo corners (EK Success); die-cut letters (QuickKutz); gift bag (Crystal Creative Products); lampshade, buttons, embroiderry floss, transparency film; envelope; cardstock

r.ā.k.

random act of kindness

On a beautiful October afternoon in 2005, Haley and her friend Angelina (instead of being bored) decided they'd do something helpful. So, they went to the neighbor's house where the big elm tree had dropped its leaves, and they raked… not because they were asked to…just because. This spontaneous act of kindness was, of course, followed by joyful rounds of repeated jumping and rolling in the big pile of leaves. Good deeds are rewarded!

Angelina

r.ā.k.

Torrey effectively echoed the soft colors of the photos in her patterned-paper choices to create a uniquely feminine fall look. Mat and mount the supporting photo series to create a sense of movement and draw the viewer's eye across the page. Roll edges of the mat on the supporting photos to resemble crunchy autumn leaves and to add just a touch of texture to the layout.

Lampshade

To cover lampshade, slowly roll shade on backside of patterned-paper remnant and trace top and bottom margin. Trim when finished and adhere paper to lampshade. Arrange leftover buttons around top and bottom edge of shade and glue in place. Wrap remaining embroidery floss around shade going in diagonal pattern from bottom buttons to top buttons. Continue until shade is completely wrapped then tie off floss on inside of shade. Cover stand with patterned paper and glue buttons around base to finish.

Coordinating gift bag and tag

Cover the front and back of the bag with patterned paper and cardstock scraps. Line the inside of the bag with contrasting color cardstock. Remove the original handles from the bag and create a diagonal handle with a single piece of left-over knotted grosgrain ribbon. For the tag, machine-stitch patterned paper to cardstock tag shape, roll edges and add a handcut sentiment to finish the tag.

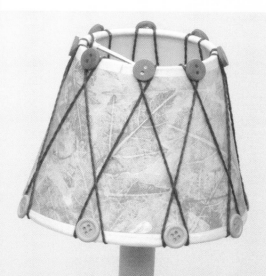

Birthday card and envelope

Machine-stitch patterned-paper scrap to the front of the card base and slightly roll edges. Adhere ribbons to the card front to create a border. Lift cut out leaf elements from the patterned paper with foam spacers to add dimension. To create the matching envelope, adhere a ribbon scraps to create border on the envelope and finish with a final patterned paper leaf.

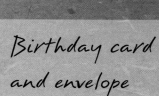

School *Daze*

by Heather

Fun and funky alphabet papers provide terrific design possibilities. Purposely choose specific letters to spell words that make great titles or sentiments on cards, or leave them alone as a playful way to accent all your paper-craft projects.

Supplies: Patterned papers (Basic Grey, Creative Imaginations, Karen Foster Design, Provo Craft); decorative brads (Karen Foster Design); rub-on letters (Making Memories); chipboard accent (Li'l Davis Designs); label maker (Dymo); metal index tab (7 Gypsies); ribbon (May Arts); decoupage medium (Plaid); frame (Walnut Hollow); card and envelope (Target); composition book; gel pen; tacky tape; staples; cardstock

Back to School

Heather's striking color choices of black and white with splashes of vibrant sherbet colors create a page that can't help but get noticed. Crop and mount ABCs, 123s and lined patterned-paper elements to help convey a "school days" theme. Add title, label-maker border and heartfelt, handwritten journaling in white for chalkboard appeal.

Embellished frame

Punch or cut patterned paper into squares and adhere collage-fashion to front of frame. Coat with decoupage medium and let dry. Decorate metal tabs with patterned paper and label-maker letters. Affix metal tabs to back of frame at top with tacky tape.

Birthday card and envelope

Cut circle from cardstock and adhere to card. Write sentiment on card and embellish with gel pen. Cut letters from patterned-paper page remnants and adhere to card. Use label maker again to create additional sentiments. Finish card with brad and ribbon. Adorn envelope with cutout patterned-paper elements from scraps and label sentiments.

Decorated journal

Cover front of composition book with contrasting strips of patterned-paper page scraps. Adhere large strip of patterned paper down right side of book front adding remaining ribbon to conceal seams. Create title with rub-on letters. Embellish with brads to complete.

Heather's tip:

Use premade embellishments sparingly. One or two well-placed elements may be all a layout needs to help bring back the fond memories.

School *Rules*

by Tricia

Whether you hand-stitch or use a machine, you can create an eye-catching edge along the paper mats of your layout. Then with needle in hand, stitch up fun album accents or a bookmark that's great for giving. Now, where's that sewing basket?

Supplies: Patterned papers (Daisy D's, Design Originals, Li'l Davis Designs, Rusty Pickle); stickers (Creative Imaginations, EK Success); charms (All My Memories, Making Memories); chipboard letters (Li'l Davis Designs); ribbon, rickrack (Offray); embroidery floss (DMC); bulldog clip; buckles; game spinner; twill; cardstock; chipboard

School Days

What says "school" better than primary colors and math? Tricia's attention to detail creates a layout that definitely makes the grade. Use patterned paper that looks just like a child's workbook and journaling on a check-out card found in library books to help convey the school theme. Create a photo mat out of composition book-style paper, hand-stitching and a charm to be reminiscent of favorite school supplies.

Accordion-fold album

Cut two pieces of chipboard into tall rectangles for front and back cover of book. Cover chipboard rectangles with patterned-paper remnants from page. Create accordion pages by folding strip of cardstock into four panels. Adhere patterned-paper scraps to front of each panel leaving top open to create pockets. Decorate pages and cover of book with leftover rub-ons, patterned paper, stickers and ribbon. Make simple cardstock tags punched with holes and tied with bits of ribbon. Mount photos onto tags and slip into pockets.

Tricia's tip:

Raid your stash of office supplies for fun embellishments to complement your layouts and your paper crafts.

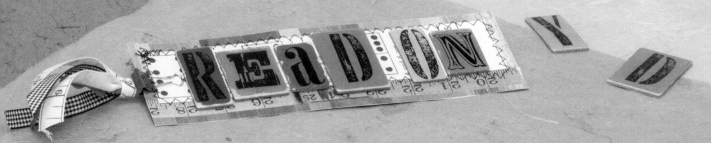

Decorative bookmark

Adhere two contrasting strips of patterned-paper scraps back to back. Add more patterned-paper strips to front and machine-stitch around paper elements. Affix chipboard letters to front. Tie remaining ribbons and rickrack to one end of bulldog clip. Attach decorated clip to end of bookmark to complete.

Grandparent *Love*

by Shannon

A single paper flower may be all you need for a simple accent on a layout, book or card. For more wow appeal, fill an entire area to create your own field of blooms.

Supplies: Patterned papers, epoxy stickers, frames, ruler book (Junkitz); photo corners (Making Memories); screw brads (Karen Foster Design); ribbon (American Crafts, Offray); chipboard letters (Heidi Swapp); letter stickers (Mustard Moon); wire word (Creative Imaginations); paper flowers (Prima); wood art (Basic Grey); journaling card (Fashion Victim); envelope; cardstock; chipboard

Create Memories

Shannon combines an oversized black-and-white photo and muted colors to create this vintage-style layout that is artistic, warm and inviting. Use metallic accents for a sharp masculine contrast against a soft yet weathered background. Adhere transparent letter stickers to create a translucent title that blends in with the background for a subtle effect.

Door hanger

Cut large circle out of chipboard, cardstock and patterned-paper scraps. Adhere cardstock circle to back of chipboard and patterned-paper circle to front. Cut smaller circle from cardstock and mat with contrasting color. Affix leftover paper flowers to smaller circle with brads. Adhere contrasting strip of cardstock through circle near bottom. Add ribbon ends to create arrow look. Decorate with ribbon and wooden accent stick. Create title from chipboard letters. Poke holes near top of hanger on either side, thread ribbon through holes and knot ends to create hanging loop.

Brag book

Cover front of each page in premade book with cardstock. Add photos, patterned paper elements, ribbons, brads, stickers and embellishments from page remnants as desired to each page. Cover front and back cover of book with patterned-paper scraps. Decorate cover with ribbon, wire word, paper flower and wood accent stick. Add chipboard letters and written strip for title.

Grandparent's Day card and envelope

Fold cardstock to create card base. Adhere matted cardstock circle to card. Affix brads and ribbon across circle element. Print sentiment on cardstock and mat with patterned-paper scraps. Apply leftover stickers, chipboard letters and printed sentiment to complete. Decorate front of envelope with matted patterned-paper rectangles, printed sentiment, paper flower and brad. Tie with remaining ribbon for the finishing touch.

Birthday *Flair*

by Heather

You know that jar of spare buttons hanging around? Dust it off and use these round wonders to dress up a little-girl layout or decorate a frame. With just a few, you can add simple elegance to a special card.

Supplies: Patterned papers (SEI); ribbon (Michaels); buttons (Junkitz); letter stickers (American Crafts); number '5' (A2Z Essentials); acrylic paint; cardstock; rickrack; pen; staples; wooden frame; clear lacquer

turning

5

grown with love

It is so hard to believe you are 5 already! Time sure does fly! We love you our sweet 5 year old!

Turning 5

Heather's layout captures a perfect glimpse of a little girl's life. Select colors and patterns to create a softly feminine palette to showcase your photos. Use strong horizontal lines to contrast with the vertical photo, making it pop off the page. Add an oversized number for an interesting element that does not overpower the page and buttons and ribbon for homespun appeal.

Greeting card and envelope

Start with a folded cardstock card base. Affix leftover ribbon and rickrack across bottom of card with staples. Adhere wide strip of pink patterned paper across card. Attach letter stickers and cutout word to strip. Cut out flower shapes from patterned paper used on page, glue buttons in centers and adhere to card. To finish, staple small piece of ribbon scrap to letter on front of card. Decorate envelope to match using cardstock, ribbon, punched flower and buttons.

Heather's Tip:

Combine just a few strips of patterned paper and ribbon on cardstock to create an effective and unique background for any remnant art.

Monogram frame

Create this frame by adhering patterned-paper remnants to background of frame. Adorn sides with bits of ribbon and buttons. Glue remaining rickrack to top and bottom of frame window. Cut out letter and flower from cardstock, coat with clear lacquer. Tie ribbon on letter and adhere to frame. Trim petals of flower to align with frame's window and adhere to frame.

Country *Pride*

by Torrey

A little goes a long way when you take leftover gingham fabrics and tear them into strips. You should have plenty to use on your layouts and home décor for a down-home, country appeal.

Supplies: Patterned papers (K & Company); corrugated paper (Paper Company); chipboard letters (Making Memories); wooden letters, wooden memo holder (Michaels); crackle medium (Rubber Stampede); acrylic paint; fabric; wheat stalks; wire mesh; brads; stamping ink; staples; paint can; pencil; cardstock

State Fair

Torrey uses textures, colors, fabrics and natural elements to breathe a comfortably worn country feel into her layout. Start with patterned-paper blocks layered on a corrugated background. Rub sandpaper and distressing ink on photos to tone down the stark white of the photos to further the overall weathered appearance of the page. Apply crackle paint to title letters for more of a weathering effect. It even works on paper, as shown here.

Altered paint can

Adhere patterned-paper page remnants around paint can. Wrap can with wire mesh and tie together on back with fabric strip to secure. Glue wheat stalks to can front. Tie can with fabric strip. Cover top of paint can with patterned paper and tie remaining fabric strips all along entire length of handle to complete.

Note holder

Cover outside of wooden memo holder with patterned-paper scraps and strip of corrugated paper. Print letters on cardstock and cut into strip, ink edges and adhere around holder. Paint leftover chipboard letter with acrylic paint and crackle medium according to manufacturer's directions. When dry, gently rub with brown ink to distress. Double mat letter on patterned paper then on corrugated paper and adhere to holder. Stamp chicken image on pieces of cardstock cropped to fit inside holder. Tie fabric bow on pencil to include with holder.

Harvest *of Plenty*

by Kathy

With a little creativity, an ordinary silk flower accent can become extraordinary. Echo the petals with pretty, looped ribbon embellished with a tag or spice one up with a bevy of buttons.

Supplies: Patterned papers (Bo-Bunny Press, Crossed Paths, Daisy D's, K & Company, Rocky Mountain Scrapbook Co.); rub-on letters, date stamp (Making Memories); paint chip (PM Designs); metal stickers, rickrack, twill (Creek Bank Creations); decorative brads, charms (Queen & Co.); fabric tab (Scrapworks); border sticker (Stamping Station); ribbons (Offray); die-cut letters (Sizzix); decoupage medium (Plaid); embroidery floss (DMC); buttons; photo turns; denim pocket; belt loops; chipboard; silk flower; bottle caps; metal-rimmed tags; cardstock; cardboard box; stamping ink; acrylic paint; transparency; card and envelope

Carving the Pumpkin

Kathy's choice of a strong complementary color scheme infuses her layout with energy. Use a brown background to create a neutral palate that grounds and anchors the layout perfectly. Pull touches of orange sprinkled all over the layout to bring out the pumpkins in the photos without overwhelming the page. Accent with denim, ribbon, buttons and flower for fresh seasonal appeal.

Kathy's tip:

By cutting twill into short pieces and securing frayed edges with a brad rather than wrapping it around to the back of the page, you can make it go farther on your remnant art.

Tag album and box

Cover both inside and outside of box with patterned paper from page. Adorn the front of box with paper strip and rub-ons. Add ribbon ties, cloth tab, silk flower and buttons from page leftovers. To create the accordion book that nests inside the box, cut 10 identically sized/shaped tags from different patterned papers so that tags will fit inside box. Cut strip of cardstock and fold into five panels, accordion-style, to same width as tags. Adhere tags to front and back of folded cardstock strip. Embellish each tag with additional photos, stickers, rub-ons, journaling blocks, buttons, ribbon and twill as desired.

Birthday card and envelope

Adhere two pieces of inked patterned-paper scraps to front of card and affix ribbon to conceal paper seam. Cut circles from contrasting colors of paper; ink edges and randomly adhere. Attach decorative brads along edge. Handcut patterned-paper monogram letter, tie letter with ribbon and adhere. Use leftover rub-on letters to create sentiment on twill and attach with brad. Ink edges of card to complete. Make the coordinating envelope by adhering inked patterned paper scrap, circular piece of contrasting paper and border stickers to envelope.

Halloween *Disguise*

by Shannon

Combine paint with foam stamps for a multitude of creative uses. Stamp a border on a greeting card, add a subtle hint of color on a wall canvas, or be bold—try it on your photos.

Supplies: Patterned papers (Karen Foster Design, Reminisce); buttons, printed twill, jump rings, brads, jelly accents (Junkitz); rub-on letters (Scrapworks); ribbon (Offray); foam stamps (Making Memories); canvas (Canvas Concepts); pen; acrylic paint; wire; clear lacquer; cardstock

It's so hard to believe that this dog costume belonged to his daddy once upon a time. And now Oliver loves to wear it for no reason at all. 2005

Oliver James

The Costume

By turning her photos to black-and-white, Shannon turns the focus toward the subject of her photos on this clever Halloween page. Mount all page elements on a diagonal slant to add visual interest and effectively lead the viewer's eyes across the page. Uniquely displaying elements at angles lends to the balance and unity that can make a layout striking.

Decorated canvas

Paint front of canvas with black acrylic paint. Paint sides, top and bottom with orange paint. Adhere strips of patterned paper down front of canvas. Wrap wire across top. Glue printed twill along top and bottom edge. Stamp pattern down right side of canvas and glue buttons down left side. Handcut jack-o'-lantern shape and paint edges black. Coat with clear lacquer and adhere to canvas.

Shannon's tip:

Push your creativity when using leftover page supplies on other crafts. You may discover a unique presentation that will be stunning on a page!

Halloween card and envelope

Fold cardstock to create card base. Cut window in leftover piece of patterned paper slightly smaller than card front. Brush edges of window with acrylic paint. Stamp image onto contrasting patterned-paper scrap and adhere behind window. Cut cardstock frame and tie remaining printed twill around bottom of frame adorned with jelly accent. Mount frame over window. Stamp designs along card edges with foam stamp. Cover envelope with patterned paper scraps. Decorate with additional strips of patterned paper and stamped pattern images.

Money gift card holder

Fold cardstock into long rectangle. Cut top right edge off on diagonal. Adhere folded cardstock along three sides leaving right side open. Cover front of holder with leftover patterned paper. Adorn with remaining buttons and wrap wire around body of holder. Use rub-on letters to create sentiment. Finish holder by adding Halloween jelly accent.

Halloween *Antics*

by Kathy

Bold, black lettering takes on instant depth when matted with a bright color on a layout. But the same letters when used unmatted have a whole different look added to a vibrant gift box or tag set.

Supplies: Patterned papers (Karen Foster Design, Queen & Co.); decorative brads, license plate, buckle, enamel letters (Karen Foster Design); brads, label holder, letter brads, photo turns, charms (Queen & Co.); letter stickers (American Crafts); leather border (Li'l Davis Designs); ribbons (Offray); rub-ons (Making Memories); label maker (Dymo); letter stamps, decoupage medium (Plaid); stamping ink; event tickets; papier-mâché box; cardstock

Darth Vader

Kathy's choice of brightly colored embellishments resembles Halloween candy. Couple that with bold patterns and you get a layout that is full of eye candy! Note how the perspective on the focal photo produces a great 3-D effect. Add title on a folded card that hides journaling to complete the design.

Gift box

Cover the top and bottom of a papier-mâché box with a variety of patterned-paper scraps. Add leftover stickers, event tickets, ribbon and alpha charms to customize. Finish the box with pre-stitched trim around the bottom edge of box and on corners of lid.

Set of gift tags

Cut out different cardstock tag shapes from scraps and decorate as desired using remaining patterned papers, ribbon, charms, etc. Add sentiments or labels to adapt tags for any occasion or theme desired. Vary word choices and color combinations according to theme. Punch holes in the tops of each tag and tie with bits of ribbon to finish.

Give *Thanks*

by Tricia

The worn, weathered feel of distressed papers works perfectly in this Thanksgiving layout. That same appeal can be carried into other crafts, such as cards and tags, by generously using your ink pads and sandpapers.

Supplies: Patterned papers (Daisy D's); die-cut letters (QuicKutz); buttons (Making Memories); walnut ink, distress ink (Ranger); border stickers (EK Success); mini brads (Creative Impressions); stitching stamp (Hero Arts); ribbon (Offray); clipboard (Saunders); silk flowers; stamping ink; mini clothespins; safety pins; paper clips; cardstock; paper bag; calendar

Giving Thanks Family Style

Tricia's layout has true homespun appeal. Use warm, rich colors and distressed papers to give your page that "lived in" look. Apply fabric-print paper and a stitched-image stamp throughout the layout to create a handmade feel. Create a recipe card journaling block and add ribbon, buttons and floral accents to complete the look.

Altered clipboard

Cover clipboard with strips of patterned paper and border stickers from page remnants. Use stitching stamp on seams. Tie two pieces of leftover knotted ribbon around clipboard. Create title from recipe card decorated with stickers, buttons and stamped sentiment. Adorn clipboard with scrap ribbons, silk flowers and buttons. Attach notes to ribbons using paper clips, safety pins and mini clothespins. Place calendar under clip. Finish project by inking raw surfaces of clipboard.

Thanksgiving card and envelope

Create card base from folded cardstock. Cover with patterned-paper scraps and stamp with stitching image. Adhere die-cut letters to form sentiment. Stamp additional sentiment on cardstock and cut into tag shape. Glue leftover ribbon, silk flower and button on card to finish. Make this unique envelope out of the bottom of a paper bag by cutting to size and folding to create flap. Stamp with stitched images and adhere ribbon, silk flower and button to complete.

Coordinating gift tag

Cut tag shape from cardstock. Cover tag with patterned-paper scraps, adding contrasting paper strip to left side of tag. Stamp with stitching image. Adhere die-cut letters to tag. Adorn with remaining ribbon, buttons and silk flower. Finish with tied ribbon through punched hole in top of tag.

WINTER

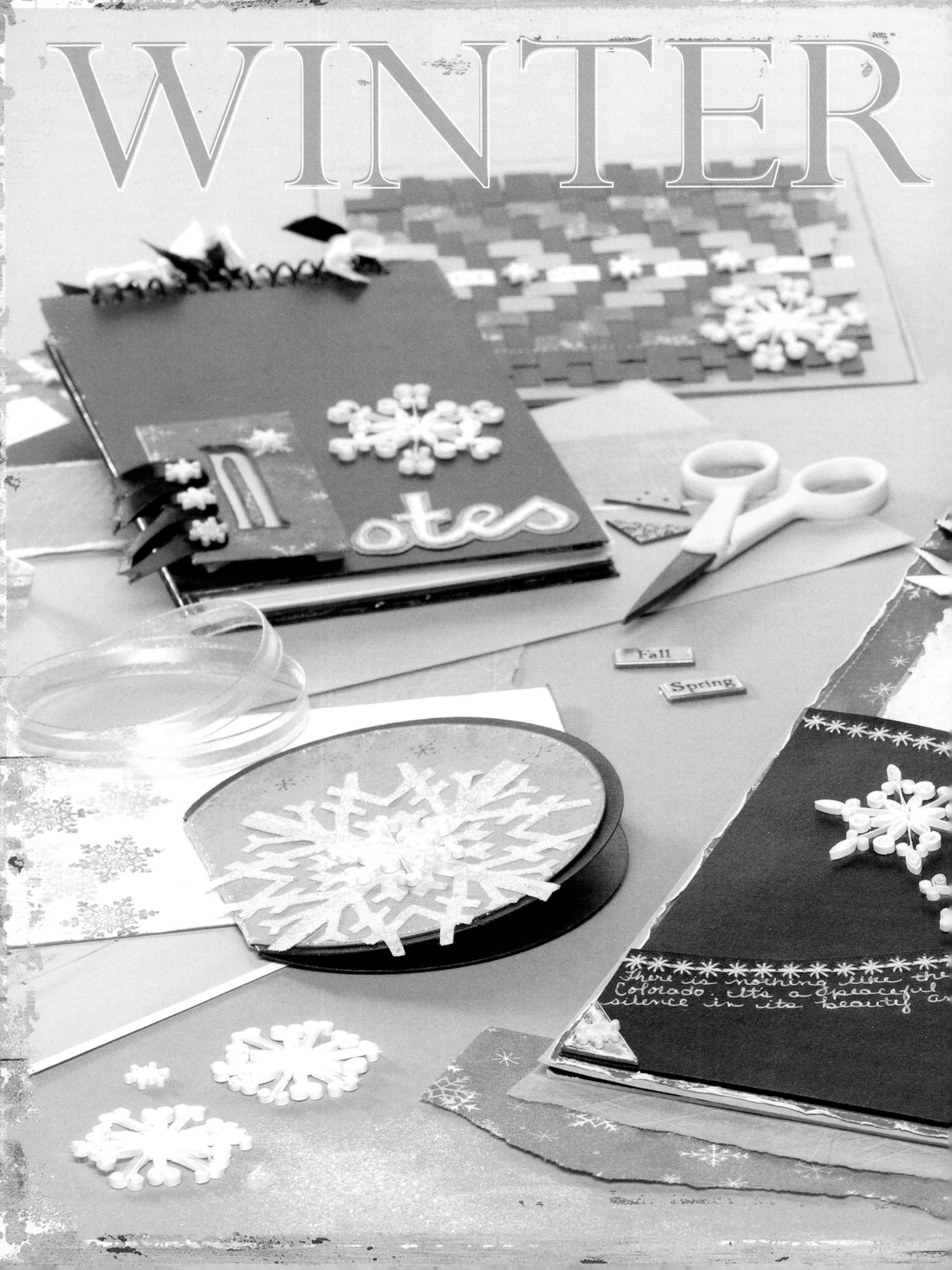

Winter brings with its arrival playful days spent frolicking in the snow and evenings curled up with hands wrapped around steaming mugs of hot cocoa. The temperatures have fallen, the days are shorter and our desires turn to warm, cozy fires and fuzzy slippers. We celebrate the holidays, look forward to a new year with all its promise and watch as the world turns white with frosty snow. Look through this chapter and you will find countless ideas created to inspire your festive winter layouts and paper creations.

nature's beauty

Winter *Wonders*

by Heather

Scraps of ribbon are just as versatile as scraps of patterned paper. Mix plaids, stripes and polka dots together to create eye-catching borders on your layouts, on the top of your bookmark or to give a finishing touch to a greeting card.

Supplies: Patterned papers (Autumn Leaves, Creative Imaginations); ribbons (Li'l Davis Designs, May Arts, Offray); epoxy stickers, twill (Creative Imaginations); buttons (Junkitz); art canvas (Canvas Concepts); rickrack; cardstock; envelope

winter BEAUTY

I took these pictures on Christmas morning before everyone was awake and all the excitement started. It was so quiet and peaceful and I just sat and reflected on the beauty and the true meaning we celebrate this day. Thank you lord for such a gift! 2005

Winter Beauty

The first thing that strikes the viewer about this wintry layout is Heather's choice of colors. Use paper and embellishments not usually associated with winter, such as pastel pinks, greens and warm browns that help pull any hint of color from snowy winter scenes. Mount an oversized photo to create a photo-centric layout that is a feast for the eyes. Use a ribbon border and vertical journaling to counterbalance each other.

Decorative wall hanging

Adhere patterned-paper strips and ribbons vertically down canvas. Affix ribbon horizontally across canvas. Cut large monogram letter from patterned-paper remnants, embellish with ribbon and mat on contrasting paper using foam spacers. Fashion ribbon flowers and secure centers with brads. Glue buttons to flower centers and adhere flowers to horizontal ribbon and to monogram. Mount monogram on canvas front to finish.

Bookmark

Cut patterned paper into long rectangle shape. Adhere strips of contrasting patterned paper and ribbon across bookmark on top and bottom. Round corners of bookmark. Staple ribbons along top edge of bookmark to complete.

Celebrate card and envelope

Fold patterned paper into rectangle to form card base. Adhere strips of contrasting patterned-paper remnants horizontally to card and staple bits of ribbon along bottom edge. Cover staples and paper strip seams with ribbon, rickrack and contrasting patterned paper. Apply epoxy sticker letters to create greeting. Write a sentiment along bottom edge of card. Decorate front of premade envelope using remaining patterned paper strips and rickrack. Finish with handwritten border sentiment.

Frosty *frolic*

by Shannon

Sometimes a patterned-paper element just needs a center anchor to ground it on a layout. Here, brads the same color as the background serve that purpose and are used again as a decorative element on the CD box cover.

Supplies: Patterned papers (My Mind's Eye); snowflake frame, mailbox letters (Making Memories); ribbon (Offray); acrylic snowflakes (Heidi Swapp); acrylic bubbles (Magic Scraps); decoupage medium (Plaid); papier-mâché star (Michaels); CD box (junk mail); acrylic paint; brads; cardstock; transparency

Snow

By combining both black-and-white and color photos, Shannon creates playful energy on her layout. Use big, colorful patterned-paper elements along the top and bottom of the page to counterbalance the weight of the photo arrangement. Hide journaling behind the photos so as not to detract from the cohesive feel of the layout. Add acrylic snowflakes, snowflake frame and mailbox title letters to complete the design.

CD box and album

Paint CD box inside and out with acrylic paint and let dry. Cover front and inside of box with patterned-paper remnants. Adorn front with leftover brads, ribbon and mail-box letters. Cut two strips of cardstock and accordion-fold strips into thirds. Overlap one section of each strip and adhere together. Add photos and hand-journaling to front and back of each page panel. Affix small ribbon loops on edge of front panel. Glue back of last panel to inside of CD box.

Star ornament

Tear patterned paper scraps into small pieces and collage on front and back of papier-mâché star. Glue paper strip on all sides of star. Coat entire star with decoupage medium and let dry. Thread ribbon through holes in star and knot ends. Adhere cutout circular element to middle of star front with brad in center.

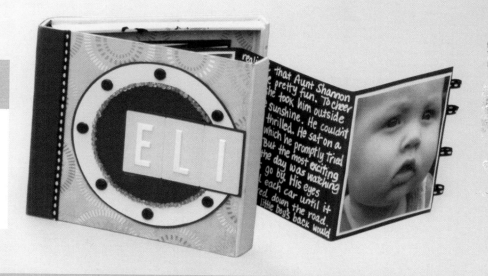

Holiday card and envelope

Fold cardstock into long rectangular card base. Affix patterned-paper scraps and printed transparency across top. Cut circles from remaining patterned paper and attach to card front with brads. Create coordinating envelope from cardstock. Paint acrylic snow-flake elements and glue to front of envelope. Adhere strips of patterned paper along bottom and side of envelope. Coat entire front of envelope with decoupage medium. While still wet, press acrylic bubbles into decoupage medium.

Snow Play

by Heather

A multipack of different-shaped metal-rimmed tags can add a playful element to your layouts and paper crafts. Mix shapes and sizes with different whimsical rub-ons applied to the vellum insets for a peekaboo effect.

Supplies: Patterned papers (7 Gypsies, Autumn Leaves); stamps (Wendi Speciale Designs); eyelet tape, brads (Junkitz); metal-rimmed tags (Making Memories); letters (A2Z Essentials); rub-ons (Autumn Leaves); decorative tape (Heidi Swapp); ribbons (May Arts, Michaels); wooden box (A.C. Moore); stamping ink; cardstock

Playing for hours in the snow

Having a little taste of snow

Making snow angels

Such a fun time in Ohio

Play

What's Heather's recipe for wintertime fun? Take one kid in a goofy hat, a puffy coat and gloves, add snow and let loose! Use soft pastel colors to play against stark black-and-white photo backgrounds. Create a playfully feminine layout with a modern feel with retro patterns such as argyle, paisley and polka dots. Complete the unabashedly playful look with patterned paper- and ribbon-adorned title and brad-fastened journaling strips.

Decorated gift box and tag

Cover box with horizontal strips of patterned-paper remnants, ribbon and eyelet trim. Tie rub-on-decorated tags to eyelet trim with leftover ribbon. Cover box lid with patterned-paper scraps. Create matching tag out of cardstock. Adorn tag with rub-ons and hand-drawn elements. Tie additional ribbon around box and lid as a finishing touch.

Artist trading card

Cut cardstock to size and adhere patterned-paper scraps to cardstock base. Decorate card front with strips of patterned paper, stamped paper and ribbon. Embellish tag with remaining rub-ons and ribbon; attach to card. Add hand-drawn border to complete.

Frosty *Days*

by Tricia

Glass pebbles can enhance and magnify lots of different things on your page design or mini books, but think outside of the box, too. Use them as decorative feet on a pretty gift box anyone would treasure.

Supplies: Patterned papers (Basic Grey, Rusty Pickle); rub-ons, word charms, metal charms, foam stamps, safety pins (Making Memories); brads (Creative Impressions, Daisy D's,); charm, papier-mâché box (Michaels); ribbon (Offray); wooden letters (Li'l Davis Designs); embroidery floss (DMC); file folder book kit (Hot Off The Press); canvas; glass pebbles; dominoes; mitten clasps; rickrack

Rosy Cheeks
Crunch Snow
Fast Sleds
Warm Mittens
Brisk Breeze
Bright Sun
Steamy Breath
Steep Hills
Big Smiles

Much Fun!

Snow Much Fun

Tricia uses traditional holiday paper colors of red and green mixed with snowy blue to create her high-energy layout. Create diagonal title and journaling strips for eye-catching elements that frame the focal photo. Add metallic charms and ribbons to mitten clasp for a fun border. Magnify a theme accent with glass pebbles. Use game pieces for accents and as clever, cryptic subjournaling.

File-folder book

Adhere patterned-paper remnants to front and back of each file-folder page. Decorate pages with die-cut shapes, ribbon, charms and additional patterned-paper elements. Add printed journaling and photos to pages. Paint inside of front and back cover of book. Adhere decorative elements including stamped tiny squares of canvas to create title. Assemble book with loose-leaf rings. To finish, tie leftover bits of ribbon to binding rings.

Tricia's tip:

Use double-sided patterned paper to double your choices and make using your scraps twice the fun!

Decorated box

Cover box and lid with patterned-paper scraps. Glue glass pebbles to bottom of box for feet. Adhere ribbon around domino and glue domino to top of lid. Add safety pin and charm to domino's ribbon. Finish box with remaining rickrack and ribbon around edge of lid.

Cozy Comfort

by Torrey

When winter's chill is in the air, find warmth in the use of velvet accents. Elegant red velvet ribbon can adorn a layout or wall hanging. Also try heat-stamping velvet for a textured touch of class.

Supplies: Patterned papers (Anna Griffin, Close To My Heart, K & Company); ribbon slides (Maya Road); brass charms (Boutique Trims); die-cut leaves (Spellbinders Paper Arts); spiral rubber stamp (Rubber Stampede); berry spray (Jo-Ann Stores); ribbon (Jo-Ann Stores, Offray, Wrights); trim (Offray); wood plaques (Hobby Lobby); envelope (Canson); rounder punch; black foam core; cardstocks

There's nothing better than a cup of cocoa on a cold winter's day. It's like wrapping up in a warm cozy blanket, but even better. After years and years of trial and effort, I've finally come up with what many people think is the perfect recipe for cocoa. If you ask nicely, I just might share it with you.

Cocoa

Torrey's layout is as rich and inviting as the cup of cocoa it features. Use richly colored paper, antiqued metal embellishments and velvety ribbon to transform a layout into a cozy and elegant mix of patterns and textures. Heat-stamp velvet to create a beautiful backdrop for a focal photo. Handcut an ornate title to top off this feast for the eyes.

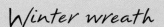

Winter wreath

Die cut paper leaves from page remnants and gently bend their edges with your fingers to give dimension. Affix onto a foam core circle. Add handcut leaf shapes from heat-stamped velvet. Finish the project by gluing sections of berry twigs around the wreath. Add a looped piece of ribbon at the top to act as a hanging loop.

Live, Laugh, Love plaque

Begin with three plain, unfinished wooden plaques. Cover the face of each plaque with patterned-paper scraps and adhere coordinating paper strips to the beveled edges. To hide the seams on the plaques, glue leftover braided trim around each facet. Adorn the face of each plaque with handcut cardstock words affixed to velvet ribbon scraps. Join the plaques together vertically with a long piece of velvet ribbon adhered to the back of each plaque. Metal embellishments between each plaque add the finishing touch.

Torrey's tip:

To conserve expensive ribbon and fabric while making it appear that there is an abundance of ribbon on a page, use short lengths and hide the ends under photos or page elements.

Nippy *Night*

by Kathy

When you start with a layout about family game night, it's easy to carry that playful appeal onto your paper crafts. Use domino game pieces, bright colors and snippets of ribbon to create fun and clever greeting cards or bookmarks.

Supplies: Patterned papers (Imagination Project, My Mind's Eye, Provo Craft); letter stickers (Sticker Studio); foam stamps (Li'l Davis Designs); rub-ons (Making Memories); chicken stickers (Crafts Etc); epoxy stickers (Creative Imaginations); ribbon (Offray); photo corners (3L); label tape (Dymo); decoupage medium (Plaid); transparency; dominoes; acrylic paint; stamping ink; staples; paint can; cardstock; card and envelope

CHICKEN foot

ISAAC

nov 20 05

HAIDEN

What started as a fun game we played at the beach soon turned into a family night game favorite. Everyone in the family can play this game and when the weather turns cold, the dominoes come out and we all dive into a family game of CHICKEN FOOT!

Chicken foot

Kathy's signature use of bright-colored patterned papers bring a seemingly calm winter's night indoor activity to life with energy. Use tongue-in-cheek humor on the layout to create a playful tone. Mount black-and-white photos and page elements to punctuate the layout in stark contrast. Add title using stamped images and letter stickers. Complete with actual game pieces to accentuate the game-night theme.

Survival kit paint can

Wrap paint can with horizontal strips of patterned-paper remnants. Adhere leftover ribbon to conceal paper seams and adorn with dominoes. Cover can lid with patterned paper decorated with sticker title. Tie ribbons along handle. Make tag from patterned-paper-covered cardstock. Embellish tag with leftover rub-on letters and stickers. Fill can with small games, deck of cards, DVDs, CDs and other fun distractions.

Greeting card and envelope

Cut patterned-paper scraps to desired size. Ink edges, add photo corners, mat on contrasting patterned paper and adhere to card. Create title for card using leftover letter stickers and label tape. Staple ribbon remnants along top edge of card to finish. Cover front of envelope with additional patterned-paper scraps, stickers and label-tape sentiments to complete.

Bookmark

Cut a strip of patterned paper and staple remaining ribbon in a loop at the top. Ink edges of bookmark. Create title with letter stickers.

Holiday *Magic*

by Courtney

Paper choices don't have to be a chore when you buy coordinating lines of paper. The work of matching prints and colors is already done for you. So, don't be afraid to mix it up on your layouts, tags and more.

Supplies: Patterned papers, letter stickers (Basic Grey); ribbon (Offray); buttons (Junkitz); embroidery floss (DMC); rub-ons (Autumn Leaves); stamping ink; cardstock; puzzle pieces; envelope

every little girl should feel like a princess especially on christmas

CHRISTMAS

PRINCESS

Christmas Princess

Sometimes a photo just speaks for itself as this photo of Courtney's little princess does. To create balance in a layout, use bold geometric shapes to counterbalance an offset, oversized photo. Keep the page embellishments at a minimum to bring your photo into the limelight.

Tag card and envelope

Glue together two pieces of patterned-paper remnants back to back; fold into tall rectangle shape and cut off upper corners to form tag-shaped card. Cover card with inked patterned-paper elements. Adorn with handwritten sentiment. Punch hole in top of card and tie with ribbon scrap. Cover front of envelope with patterned paper. Decorate with patterned-paper rectangles and circles. Complete the project with a floss-tied button and handwritten sentiment.

Puzzle-piece ornament

Cut desired-size ring from cardstock scrap to act as base for ornament. Cover puzzle pieces with various patterned paper remnants. Add photos, button and printed sentiment on puzzle pieces. Arrange and glue covered puzzle pieces to cardstock ring base. Finish ornament with leftover ribbon bow and loop for hanging.

Courtney's tip:

Don't throw away games and puzzles that have missing parts! Salvage the pieces to use as embellishments for scrapbooking and paper crafts.

Personalized gift tags

Create bases for tags from rectangles and squares of patterned-paper scraps. Adorn front of each tag as desired with patterned-paper elements, monograms, buttons and letter stickers. Punch a hole in each tag and tie with festive ribbon to finish.

Christmas *Joy*

by Heather

Creating a patchwork of patterned paper is a fun and easy way to accent a layout or paper crafts. Cut the paper in strips or into squares for a variety of festive looks. What a great way to stretch your paper stash!

Supplies: Patterned papers (A2Z Essentials); charms (Making Memories); rickrack, ribbon (May Arts); printed canvas (My Mind's Eye); staples; clear lacquer; gift bag; cardstock; cardboard

stockings | presents | eve

Christmas is such a wonderful magical time and this year was no different. We spent our holidays in Ohio with my family and had a memorable time with lots of memories made. Kiersten gets more excited each year in her expectation and it was wonderful to watch her this year. And she is always quick to tell us that it is baby Jesus that we are celebrating. We are so proud of her and look forward to the many traditions she will carry on with her as she grows and starts her own family.

Stockings, Presents, Eve

Heather turns down the lights in order to turn up the "wow" factor of her dramatic photos. Use an enlarged photo to pull double-duty as both a border design element and as a focal photo. Give traditional holiday colors of red and green a vibrant new makeover in the form of fuchsia and lime. Add synergy to the layouts with fun, bold patterns.

Heather's tip:

Create your own interesting titles and embellishments to use on creative paper crafts by downloading unique free fonts from Internet Web sites.

Holiday wall hanging

Cut desired-size square out of cardboard. Cover cardboard with small squares of patterned-paper remnants to create a frame effect. Adhere printed sentiment to center of wall hanging. Coat entire front with clear lacquer and let dry. Glue leftover charms to front for decoration. Adhere ribbon on all edges of wall hanging.

He who has not
Christmas
in his heart
will never find
it under a tree

Holiday gift bag and tag

Cover all sides of bag with vertical strips of patterned-paper scraps. Staple remaining rickrack on sides along top and bottom edges. Replace existing handle with leftover, knotted ribbon. For tag, cut circle from patterned-paper scraps and mat with cardstock. Affix cardstock strips randomly to front with staples. Write sentiment on cardstock strips. Punch hole in top of tag, decorate with remaining charm and ribbon.

To:
From:

Christmas

Yuletide *Splendor* by Nic

Add a new level of dimension to your layouts with textured acrylic letters. But don't stop there—they provide great design elements for tag books and gift boxes as well.

Supplies: Patterned papers (Scenic Route Paper Co.); rub-ons (Basic Grey); ribbon (Li'l Davis Designs); acrylic letters (Go West Studios); mesh (Magic Mesh); stamping ink; photo corners; cardstock

Christmas Joy

Nic is the queen of machine-stitching on her pages, and this holiday layout is no exception. Layer and stitch patterned papers with ribbons and mesh for a textured background. Use graphic design elements to give the layout a modern feel. The stitching provides a classic touch of handmade appeal.

Nic's tip:

Even the most basic boxes found in everyday life can be altered using a few page remnants. It's easy to make them into absolutely stunning gift packages.

Embellished gift box and tag

Adhere sewn and matted patterned-paper remnants to each side of green box. Glue leftover ribbon around entire box and box lid. Embellish box front with rub-on and acrylic-letter sentiment mounted on a scrap of mesh under a handmade label holder. Fashion a paper bow out of strips of patterned paper and acrylic charms; glue to lid. Create tag from sewn patterned-paper scrap matted on cardstock and cut into tag shape. Add rub-on letter sentiments. Punch hole in top of card and tie with ribbon to complete.

Tag book

Cut several identically sized and shaped pieces of cardstock to create base for book. Cover each page front with patterned-paper remnants adorned with machine-stitching. Print journaling blocks on cardstock and adhere to pages. Decorate other pages with additional bits of inked patterned paper, ribbon, acrylic letters and rub-ons. Adhere matted photos to pages, using photo corners on a few. Decorate cover using printed image and rub-ons as title. Punch hole in top of each tag page and tie with leftover ribbon and attach acrylic charms.

New Year *Cheer*

Supplies: Patterned papers (Basic Grey, Daisy D's, Scenic Route Paper Co.); beads (Blue Moon Beads); rub-on letters (Making Memories); ribbon (Offray); bamboo tiles; glitter; chipboard; stamping ink; card base and envelope; cardstock; vellum; mini brads; wire; tacky tape

by Torrey

Wirework doesn't need to be fussy. Go wild with free-form wire shapes to accentuate your layout and paper crafts. Keep bending and shaping until you get just that right twist for whatever you're making.

Happy New Year

Torrey takes a long-standing family tradition and chronicles it in her uniquely festive layout. Use black matting atop patterned-paper blocks to make a horizontal photo seem to pop right off the page. Adhere fun free-form wire and bead embellishments to give the layout a ready-to-party feel.

New Year's card and envelope

Cover card base with patterned-paper remnants. Adhere left-over ribbon vertically down card. Cut circle from patterned-paper scrap; cover with tacky tape and coat with glitter. Mount on ribbon. Apply rub-on letters to matted patterned-paper shape to create title. Apply rub-on numbers to bamboo tiles. Connect tiles with free-form wire and attach. Decorate envelope with patterned-paper strip, rub-ons and glitter glue.

Desktop calendar

Fold chipboard strip in half to create table-tent shape. Cut 1" off bottom of back to angle calendar slightly backward and provide stability. Cover both sides of chipboard with patterned paper scraps. Cut a long strip of patterned paper; adhere across bottom front of chipboard, around sides and adhere on back to provide a brace for calendar. Print calendar pages, cut to uniform size and staple together. Glue calendar pages to front. Cover top of calendar pages with patterned paper strip. Adorn front with remaining rub-on numbers, brads and patterned paper pinwheels.

Valentine *Kiss*

by Amy

Even though there's frost on the windows, look forward to spring with these lively, romantic valentine colors. Then keep that feeling in bloom with home-décor projects and cards that will brighten any day.

Supplies: Patterned papers, die cuts (My Mind's Eye); ribbon (Offray); stickers (Provo Craft); brads, acrylic letters (Junkitz); rub-ons (KI Memories); metal container (Heart & Home); flower punch (Family Treasures); pencils; transparency; card base; floral foam

Will YOU be mine?

AMORE

yesterday...

The first time ever I saw your face was all it took for me to fall in love. You were there on the beach on the sand and your eyes were as bright as the sky. I never thought anyone as wonderful as you would even take a second glance in my direction.

valentine valentine **valentine** valentine

tomorrow...

Who knows where we will be in 20 years but, the one thing I **DO** know, my sweet valentine, is that I want to be sure I am with **YOU!**

today...

I love you more today than yesterday. Each day is like an adventure -- I am always excited to see how my life is enriched by having you in it.

LOVE

Will You Be Mine?

Amy uses a color-block technique to separate key elements of her layout. Print all journaling on patterned-paper blocks. Assemble page elements following the "rule of thirds" and an eye-catching visual triangle through the use of color and photo placement to create a strong and balanced layout. Complete with title and accents.

Pencil holder

Adhere matted patterned-paper strip around middle of container. Mat letter stickers and affix them along patterned-paper strip. Glue ribbon bow to center top of container. Cut floral foam to fit inside container and glue in place. Punch circles and flower shapes from patterned-paper scraps. Adhere circle centers to flowers and glue to pencil ends. Arrange pencils in floral foam.

Amy's tip:

Create your own embellishment from a paper scrap by printing text in a circle and adding a title in the middle. You will have an instant, custom-made die cut.

Valentine card and envelope

Adhere patterned-paper remnants along bottom of card. Add leftover rub-on elements, alphabet embellishments and printed sentiment. Finish card with brads. Create matching envelope from patterned-paper scraps. Adhere double-matted strip of patterned paper across front. Decorate with letter stickers and rub-on elements.

Artist trading card

Start with a scrap of patterned paper with rounded corners. Cover with a coordinating patterned-paper scrap. Embellish card front with perpendicular strips of contrasting patterned paper. Add remaining rub-on elements, alphabet pieces, brads and a handcut monogram from patterned paper. Adhere ribbon to back of card, forming loop at top.

True *Love* *by Amy*

There's nothing like a flower accent to fancy up a layout. Whether you punch them from paper or fabric yourself or pick some up at the store, you'll find a whole bouquet of different uses for these versatile, feminine blooms.

Supplies: Patterned papers, rub-ons, fabric elements (Autumn Leaves); metal letters (American Crafts); brads (Junkitz); index tab (Heidi Swapp); papier-mâché box (Michaels); cardstock

Love

Amy uses a horizontal format for her layout, an arrangement that still accommodates fairly large photos without looking crowded. Start by combining soft, romantic colors and bold graphic patterns mounted in vertical strips to create a layout that embodies both masculine and feminine qualities. Finish with title and journaling.

Accordion book

Create three identically folded paper card bases. Adhere front of one card base to back of next to create accordion. Decorate pages as desired with patterned-paper remnants and leftover metal letters, fabric elements and rub-ons. Adhere index tab on top of each page. Insert printed sentiments into tabs. Embellish cover with additional fabric elements and rub-on letters to create title. Glue ribbon to front and back cover for ties.

Amy's tip:

Vintage lace and notions are great finds at local flea markets and sales. They make beautiful accents on scrapbook pages or paper crafts and can be easily altered with inks, dyes and chalks.

Decorated gift box

Cover box with patterned-paper remnants on all sides. Adhere vertical contrasting patterned-paper strip to middle of each side. Adhere same patterned paper around edge of lid. Cover lid with patterned paper, creating mitered frame on top of lid out of contrasting patterned-paper strips. Affix remaining fabric elements to top of lid. Poke holes in right and left sides of box. Thread twill through holes; place lid on box and tie twill over lid to secure.

Additional Instructions & Credits

COVER QUIET BEAUTY

Jodi uses soft, muted tones representative of springtime on this layout to keep the focus directly on the photo. The looped ribbon flowers accented with button centers and rickrack stems add just the right feminine touch to complete the layout with simple elegance.

Jodi Amidei, Memory Makers Books
Photo: Ken Trujillo, Memory Makers

Supplies: Patterned papers (Autum Leaves); textured cardstock (Prism) ribbon (Offray); buttons (Blumenthal Lansing); die-cut letters (Spellbinders Paper Arts); brads (Making Memories) frame (discount dollar store); rickrack (unknown); card and envelope (Halcraft)

COVER FRAME

Cover frame with patterned-paper scraps creating a matted effect using orange cardstock. Add contrasting paper around edges of frame. Ink edges to cover seams. Use leftover ribbon on left side of frame and adorn with rickrack and buttons.

COVER SPIRAL NOTEBOOK

Attach remnant pieces of patterned paper and cardstock to front and back cover of small spiral notebook. Hide the seam of papers with ribbon scrap wrapped around cover. Adorn with a looped ribbon flower and button. Add small ribbon scraps tied to binding to complete.

COVER GOOD LUCK CARD AND ENVELOPE

Cover front of card base with cardstock. Free-form cut shapes from scrap patterned paper. Adhere die-cut title, rickrack, paper flower and button to decorate. Add final touches with white gel pen. Complete matching envelope by gluing flower cutout and rickrack to envelope front.

PAGE 1 NATURAL BEAUTY

Jodi's ultra-feminine layout draws its inspiration from colors and patterns one would find in interior design. Create the background of rich texture by curling the edges of thin, vertically sewn strips of patterned paper. Construct delicate title and name by hand-cutting from coordinating paper. Add silk flowers, lace, buttons and lacquered paper elements to finish.

Jodi Amidei, Memory Makers Books

Supplies: Patterned papers (7 Gypsies, Anna Griffin, Chatterbox, Daisy D's, Déjà Views, K & Company, My Mind's Eye); ribbon (Offray); buttons (Blumenthal Lansing, Junkitz); tags (Delta); beads (Beadery); paper flowers (Jo-Ann Stores); embroidery floss (Creative Impressions); photo corners (Canson); glitter glue (Duncan); die-cut letters (QuicKutz); box (Wal-Mart); frame (All Night Media); micro beads (Provo Craft); silk flowers; tacky tape; clear lacquer; embossing enamel; cardstock; card and envelope

PAGE 1 LOVE CARD AND ENVELOPE

Adhere patterned-paper scraps to cardstock base. Cover paper elements with tacky tape and press clear micro beads onto tape before adhering to card. Wrap a large slide mount with leftover patterned paper and affix to card with foam spacers. Add handwritten sentiment on cardstock strip. Die cut letters from patterened-paper scraps and glue to card for title. Adorn with leftover ribbon, lace trim and glitter glue.

PAGE 1 DECORATED FRAME

Affix torn remaining patterned-paper strips to front of frame. Ink edges of frame. Adhere inner frame cut from patterned paper to frame. Coat internal frame with clear lacquer and let dry.

PAGE 1 FLORAL DECORATED GIFT BOX

Cover a small cardboard box and lid with patterned-paper remnants. Glue silk flowers to completely cover top of lid. Glue decorative beads on bottom of box to act as base.

PAGE 3 SOFT TOUCH

Jodi captures a once-in-a-lifetime special moment between a girl and a dolphin in her playful layout. Choose marine-inspired colors to complement the feeling of the open sea. Machine-stitch strips of patterned paper to background. Add handcut dolphin accents for the perfect finishing touch.

Jodi Amidei, Memory Makers Books

Supplies: Patterned papers (Doodlebug Design, Heidi Grace Designs, KI Memories, Robin's Nest); rub-ons, die-cuts (KI Memories); ribbon (Making Memories); eyelets (Deluxe Designs); textured cardstock (DieCuts with a View); card base/envelope (Halcraft); notecard/address holder (discount store); frame (dollar store); dolphin clip art

PAGE 3 DECORATED FRAME

Cover frame with patterned paper scraps. Add strip of contrasting paper down left front of frame. Adhere strip of patterned paper around to inside and outside edges of frame. Tie leftover ribbon around left side of frame.

PAGE 3 DESK ORGANIZER

Carefully dismantle holder, removing frame and bottom support piece. Cover frame and bottom of holder with patterned-paper scraps. Adhere leftover ribbon along top and bottom edges of holder. Attach frame to front of holder and insert photo. Cover accompanying address book with leftover cardstock. Glue ribbon to front and back cover to create ties. Decorate front of address book with torn strips of paper and handcut title. Remove old cover from notebook and create new cover from remaining cardstock. Punch holes along the edge of cardstock and feed spiral binding through holes. Adorn front of notebook. Tie ribbon pieces on top spiral to complete.

PAGE 3 THANKS CARD AND ENVELOPE

Ink edges of card. Adhere crimped and inked paper strips remnants to card. Add crimped cutout element adorned with flower leftover rub-on to card. Finish card with handcut sentiment and ribbon embellishment. Decorate envelope with inked and crimped remaining paper strips and flower rub-on.

PAGE 6 GIGGLES

Jodi's choice of colors shouts "Girls Rule!" on this groovy all-girl page. Add patterned paper to background using machine-stitching. Offset a handcut title to add a playful touch. Add acrylic paint behind the transparency to softly highlight journaling. Add gold foil accents and rhinestones to add the perfect amount "bling" to finish the layout.

Jodi Amidei, Memory Makers Books
Photo: Kelli Noto, Centennial, Colorado

PAGE 6 DECORATED CAN

Cover outside of can with patterned-paper remnants. Glue scraps of rickrack on can and add leather flowers trimmed with rhinestone brads. Cover top of can in similar fashion adding folded ribbon to each flower. Glue painted wooden bead for handle on top of can.

PAGE 7 HI CARD AND ENVELOPE

To create the gilt background, adhere photo splits in checkerboard pattern to background paper remnants. Press gold foil into photo splits, gently wiping off excess. Mat checkerboard paper with contrasting patterned paper and stitch to card front. Handcut letters from patterned-paper scraps. Edge letters with gold leafing pen before affixing to torn patterned-paper strip. Finish card with leftover rhinestone and acrylic accents.

PAGE 7 PAPER BAG BOOK

Use three brightly colored gift bags to create the base for book. Lay folded bags flat on top of each other and punch two evenly spaced holes through all bags in center of stack. With leftover ribbon, tie bags together through holes to create binding. Fold in center to create book pages. Decorate the cover and each page of the book as desired using remaining patterned paper, photos, embellishments, ribbon and tags. Adhere lengths of ribbon to inside of front and back cover to create closure.

PAGES 8-9 ARTIST TRADING CARDS

Kathy Fesmire

Supplies: Patterned papers (Bo-Bunny Press, Daisy D's, Lazar Studiowerx); label letters (EK Success); enamel flower, epoxy letters (Karen Foster Design); sticker (Creek Bank Creations); ribbon (Offray); stamping ink

Amy Goldstein

Supplies: Patterned paper, die cut (My Mind's Eye); rub-ons (Autumn Leaves, KI Memories); brad (Making Memories)

Nic Howard

Supplies: Patterned paper (Scenic Route Paper Co.); ribbon (Heidi Grace Designs); decorative brad, photo turn (Queen & Co.); stamping ink; cardstock

Heather Preckel

Supplies: Patterned paper (Chatterbox); ribbon (Michaels); flower (Making Memories); rickrack; stamping ink; staples; cardstock; pen

Tricia Rubens

Supplies: Pattered paper (Daisy D's); watch face (Li'l Davis Designs); label (Dymo); screw brad (Creative Impressions); denim; buttons

Torrey Scott

Supplies: Patterned paper (Basic Grey); ribbon (Offray); die-cut letters (Spellbinders Paper Arts); transparency; cardstock; butterfly clip art

Shannon Taylor

Supplies: Patterned paper (Basic Grey); moon clip (House This); ribbon (American Crafts); brads (Junkitz); cardstock

Courtney Walsh

Supplies: Patterned paper (Autumn Leaves); paper flowers (Prima); brads (Making Memories); letter stickers (SEI); ribbon (M&J Trimming); stamping ink; cardstock

PAGE 10 SERENITY

The simplicity of Torrey's layout creates an almost Zen-like feel–from the soft, earthen colors to the simple repetitive forms, this layout exudes a sense of peace and tranquility. Create a roughly blocked background out of coordinating patterned papers matted in black. Sand and ink the edges of the photo to add a soft, worn look. Add a handcut title from coordinating patterned paper to complete.

Torrey Scott, Thornton, Colorado

Supplies: Patterned paper (Crafter's Workshop); spiral journal (Jo-Ann Stores); stamping ink; cardstock; transparency film; card/envelope

PAGE 10 SPIRAL "NOTES" BOOK

Carefully remove spiral binding. Cover front and back with remaining cardstock. Cut geometric shapes from patterned-paper scraps and adhere to front cover. Handcut title from cardstock and adhere. Replace spiral binding by starting at one end and feeding spiral through holes.

PAGE 12-13 DELICATE FLOWER

Delicate hues of periwinkle and lavender grace this beautiful layout. Fashion a patchwork background by overlapping rectangles of coordinating patterned paper. Secure each rectangle to the background by machine-stitching to cardstock. Gently curl edges to add a touch of texture. Handwrite journaling and handcut title to add a finishing elegant touch.

Jodi Amidei, Memory Makers Books
Photo: Will Smale, Copper Mountain, Colorado

Supplies: Patterned papers (Colorbök, Hot Off The Press, Paper Adventures); brads (Making Memories, Creative Impressions); die-cut letters (QuicKutz); stamps (Technique Tuesday); glitter glue (Ranger); wire (Michaels); felt pen (EK Success); candles (Midwestern Home Products); ribbon (Offray); cardstock; card/envelope; stamping ink; memo pad; chipboard

PAGE 12 CONGRATS CARD AND ENVELOPE

Cover card with patterned-paper remnants. Randomly cut various-sized rectangles from coordinating patterned-paper scraps and adhere to card. Cut out design elements from patterned paper and affix to card and adhere ribbon. Die cut letters and glue to ribbon. Lightly ink edges of card. Outline elements of card with glitter glue to finish.

PAGE 12 DECORATED CANDLES

Loosely wrap the candle with wire. Twist wire ends into coils and gently pull apart into casual spiral. To secure wire to candle, heat back of candle briefly with heat gun and firmly press wire into softened wax. Cut or punch heart shapes out of patterned paper left over from page. Adorn hearts with glitter glue. Adhere paper hearts randomly to front of candle to complete.

PAGE 13 MINI ALBUM

To make album cover, cut a long strip of cardstock scrap. Fold lower inch of strip up to create flap. Fold top of strip down so that it just tucks under flap. Cut several cardstock pages to fit inside cover. Cover front and back of each page with patterned-paper remnants. Align pages under flap of cover and punch two evenly spaced holes through all layers. Secure flap and pages with brads. Cover front cover of book with patterned-paper scraps and adorn with photo and stamped sentiment. Additional photos added to each page complete the book.

PAGE 13 TEAR-OFF MEMO BOOK

On chipboard, trace memo sheet to create base for front and back covers. Trace around end of memo stack to make chipboard spine for holder. Cut out all pieces. Lay pieces in order (cover, spine, cover) on patterned-paper strip leaving small gap between each chipboard piece. Adhere in place. Cut patterned paper a little larger all around chipboard pieces. Fold patterned paper over edges of chipboard and affix. Adhere additional strip of patterned-paper scrap to inside of cover to conceal folded edges. Adhere memo stack to inside spine with tacky tape. Fold cover over and decorate with leftover supplies as desired.

PAGE 14 VISIONS OF SPRING

Abby photo: Lucy Vander Loos, Pukekone, Auckland, New Zealand

PAGE 40-41 RELAX AND RENEW

Jodi uses lighter shades of warm colors along with sanded and distressed edges to give the page elements the illusion of being bleached by the tropical sun. Layer patterned paper for background and accentuate with circular paper element. Add journaling block to echo the lines of the photo. Create title by covering chipboard letters with patterned paper and sanding edges.

Jodi Amidei, Memory Makers Books
Photo: Will Smale, Copper Mountain, Colorado

Supplies: Patterned papers (Autumn Leaves, Chatterbox); chipboard letters (Li'l Davis Designs); ribbon, papier-mâché boxes (Michaels); cardstock; pen

PAGE 40 DECORATIVE MINI BOXES

Cover boxes and lids with contrasting patterned-paper scraps. Stack boxes and tie, package-style, with leftover ribbon into bow on top.

PAGE 40 TAGS

Cut different tag shapes from remaining cardstock. Cover tags with patterned-paper scraps and machine-stitch along edge. Gently curl edges of stitched patterned paper. Decorate tags with leftover chipboard letter, cutout paper elements and photos. Create hangers for tags using looped patterned paper or ribbon tied through punched holes.

PAGE 41 LUV U CARD AND ENVELOPE

Fold cardstock to create card base. Adhere patterned-paper remnant to card. Mat contrasting strips of patterned paper and glue on card in random pattern. Cover chipboard letters with leftover patterned paper and lightly sand edges. Mat covered letters with cardstock and mount diagonally on card. For envelope, mat strips of patterned-paper scraps and adhere along bottom edge of envelope.

PAGE 60 MEXICO

Parrot and hibiscus photos: Heidi Finger, Brighton, Colorado

PAGE 68-69 AUTUMN SPLENDOR

Jodi's choice of warm, rich autumn colors and nature-themed elements showcase this marvelous vista. Create background by stitching patterned paper to cardstock and curling the edges slightly. Add cutout elements, subtle journaling and a simple title to lend a sense of reverence completing the page.

Jodi Amidei, Memory Makers Books
Photos: Nick Nyffeler, Memory Makers Books

Supplies: Patterned papers (Close To My Heart, Karen Foster Design, Scenic Route Paper Co.); decorative brads (Queen & Co.); eyelets (Deluxe Designs); ribbon (Offray); chipboard letters (Heidi Swapp); natural ribbon (Michaels); card base/envelope (DMD); wooden box (dollar store); stamping ink; CD; cardstock

PAGE 68 THANKS CARD AND ENVELOPE

Cover card with patterned-paper remnants and ink all edges. Sand edges of photo, ink to distress and adhere to card. Set eyelets vertically along top of card. Tie scrap ribbons through eyelets. Adhere chipboard sentiment. For matching envelope, adhere inked strips of patterned-paper scraps along edge of envelope. Lightly ink edges of envelope to complete project.

PAGE 68 ALTERED CD

Cut graduated circles of patterned-paper leftovers and lightly sand edges. Adhere circles to CD. Handcut sentiment from patterned-paper scrap and glue to CD front. Cut photo into smallest circle, sand edges and adhere to CD. Cover back of CD with remaining patterned paper to finish.

PAGE 68 DECORATED BOX

Cover box and lid with contrasting patterned-paper scraps. Cut out image from remaining patterned paper and adhere to lid, cutting off any excess. Ink all edges of box and lid to add finishing touch.

PAGE 74 R.Ã.K.

Photos: Jodi Amidei, Memory Makers Books

PAGE 94-95 SILENCE, SOLITUDE

Serene monochromatic shades of blue add grace and dignity to Jodi's frosty winter layout. Add texture to frame and title by using paper paste and opal flakes. Delicate, quilled snowflake accents are a simple and beautiful complement to the layout and handwritten journaling completes the page.

Jodi Amidei, Memory Makers Books
Photo: Will Smale, Copper Mountain, Colorado

Supplies: Patterned paper (Carolee's Creations); shimmery cardstock (Paper Adventures); ribbon (Hobby Lobby); paper paste (DecoArt); quilled snowflakes (Provo Craft); snowflake buttons (Jesse James); photo corners, chipboard letters, word plaques (Making Memories); snowflake stamp (source unknown); watermark ink (Tsukineko); opal flakes (Rubba Dub Dub); acrylic paint; stamping ink; glitter; glitter glue; white gel pen; cardstock; papier-mâché box; spiral notebook;

PAGE 94 SPIRAL NOTEBOOK

Carefully remove spiral binding from notebook. Adhere cardstock scraps to front and back covers. Punch holes for binding through cardstock. Cover chipboard monogram letter with patterned-paper remnant and mount on white cardstock. Handcut remaining sentiment from patterned paper. Adhere letter and sentiment to notebook. Add additional ribbon and decorative buttons and snowflake element. Line up holes in both covers and pages and replace spiral binding. Tie ribbons onto spiral to complete.

PAGE 94 SNOWFLAKE CARD AND ENVELOPE

Fold cardstock rectangle in half to form square. Cut folded square into semi-circle shape leaving folded edge intact. Mat with contrasting color cardstock scrap. Using watermark ink, stamp snowflake images onto card. Apply glitter glue around edges of card. Handcut paper snowflake, lightly spritz with spray adhesive and sprinkle with glitter. Adhere glittered snowflake to card. Affix leftover quilled snowflake element to center of handcut snowflake. Finish card with handwritten sentiment. Decorate accompanying envelope with randomly stamped snowflake images adorned with glitter glue.

PAGE 95 "SNOW" COVERED BOX

Apply paper paste paint to box lid using palette knife. While wet, sprinkle with opal flakes and gently press into paint. Let lid dry completely according to manufacturer's directions. Cover box with patterned-paper remnants. Wrap ribbon scraps around bottom edge of box and embellish with decorative buttons.

PAGE 94 WOVEN WINTER CARD AND ENVELOPE

Cut cardstock and patterned paper into strips. Weave paper strips together using Bargello pattern and machine-stitch onto card. Add handwritten sentiment, decorative buttons and quilled snowflake to complete card. For envelope, adhere strips of patterned paper in loose weave to envelope and adorn with button. Ink edges of envelope as finishing touch.

Source Guide

The following companies manufacture products featured in this book. Please check your local retailers to find these materials, or go to a company's Web site for the latest product. In addition, we have made every attempt to properly credit the items mentioned in this book. We apologize to any company that we have listed incorrectly, and we would appreciate hearing from you.

3L Corporation
(800) 828-3130
www.scrapbook-adhesives.com

7 Gypsies
(877) 749-7797
www.sevengypsies.com

A2Z Essentials
(419) 663-2869
www.a2zessentials.com

ACCO Brands
(800) 989-4923
www.acco.com

A.C. Moore
www.acmoore.com

All My Memories
(888) 553-1998
www.allmymemories.com

All Night Media
(see Plaid Enterprises)

American Crafts
(801) 226-0747
www.americancrafts.com

American Traditional Designs®
(800) 448-6656
www.americantraditional.com

Amscan, Inc.
(800) 444-8887
www.amscan.com

Anna Griffin, Inc.
(888) 817-8170
www.annagriffin.com

Arctic Frog
(479) 636-FROG
www.arcticfrog.com

Autumn Leaves
(800) 588-6707
www.autumnleaves.com

Avery Dennison Corporation
(800) GO-AVERY
www.avery.com

Basic Grey™
(801) 451-6006
www.basicgrey.com

Bazzill Basics Paper
(480) 558-8557
www.bazzillbasics.com

Beadery®, The
(401) 539-2432
www.thebeadery.com

Berwick Offray™, LLC
(800) 344-5533
www.offray.com

Blue Moon Beads
(800) 377-6715
www.bluemoonbeads.com

Blumenthal Lansing Company
(201) 935-6220
www.buttonsplus.com

Bo-Bunny Press
(801) 771-4010
www.bobunny.com

Boutique Trims, Inc.
(248) 437-2017
www.boutiquetrims.com

Bulldog- no contact info

Canson®, Inc.
(800) 628-9283
www.canson-us.com

Canvas Concepts™
(415) 822-9202
www.canvasconcepts.com

Card Connection- see Michaels

Carolee's Creations®
(435) 563-1100
www.ccpaper.com

Chatterbox, Inc.
(208) 939-9133
www.chatterboxinc.com

Close To My Heart®
(888) 655-6552
www.closetomyheart.com

Colorbök™, Inc.
(800) 366-4660
www.colorbok.com

Crafter's Workshop, The
(877) CRAFTER
www.thecraftersworkshop.com

Crafts, Etc. Ltd.
(800) 888-0321
www.craftsetc.com

Creative Imaginations
(800) 942-6487
www.cigift.com

Creative Impressions Rubber Stamps, Inc.
(719) 596-4860
www.creativeimpressions.com

Creek Bank Creations, Inc.
(217) 427-5980
www.creekbankcreations.com

Crossed Paths™
(972) 393-3755
www.crossedpaths.net

Crystal Creative Products- no contact info

Daisy D's Paper Company
(888) 601-8955
www.daisydspaper.com

Darice, Inc.
(800) 321-1494
www.darice.com

DecoArt™ Inc.
(800) 367-3047
www.decoart.com

Déjà Views
(800) 243-8419
www.dejaviews.com

Delta Technical Coatings, Inc.
(800) 423-4135
www.deltacrafts.com

Deluxe Designs
(480) 497-9005
www.deluxedesigns.com

Design Originals
(800) 877-0067
www.d-originals.com

Destination™ Scrapbook Designs
(866) 806-7826
www.destinationstickers.com

DieCuts with a View™
(877) 221-6107
www.dcwv.com

DMC Corp.
(973) 589-0606
www.dmc.com

DMD Industries, Inc.
(800) 805-9890
www.dmdind.com

Don Mechanic Enterprises
(800) 345-8143
www.donmechanic.com

Doodlebug Design™ Inc.
(801) 966-9952
www.doodlebug.ws

Duncan Enterprises
(800) 782-6748
www.duncan-enterprises .com

Dymo
(800) 426-7827
www.dymo.com

Eberhard Faber
www.eberhardfaber.de

EK Success™, Ltd.
(800) 524-1349
www.eksuccess.com

Emagination Crafts, Inc.
(866) 238-9770
www.emaginationcrafts.com

Family Treasures®
(949) 290-0872
www.familytreasures.com

Fashion Victim- no contact info

Fiskars®, Inc.
(800) 950-0203
www.fiskars.com

Go West Studios
(214) 227-0007
www.goweststudios.com

Halcraft USA
(212) 376-1580
www.halcraft.com

Heart & Home, Inc.
(905) 686-9031
www.heartandhome.com

Heidi Grace Designs
(866) 89heidi
www.heidigrace.com

Heidi Swapp/Advantus Corporation
(904) 482-0092
www.heidiswapp.com

Hero Arts® Rubber Stamps, Inc.
(800) 822-4376
www.heroarts.com

Hobby Lobby Stores, Inc.
www.hobbylobby.com

Hot Off The Press, Inc.
(800) 227-9595
www.paperpizazz.com

House This, Inc.- no contact info

Imagination Project, Inc.
(513) 860-2711
www.imaginationproject.com

Inkadinkado® Rubber Stamps
(800) 888-4652
www.inkadinkado.com

Jesse James & Co., Inc.
(610) 435-0201
www.jessejamesbutton.com

Jo-Ann Stores
(888) 739-4120
www.joann.com

Junkitz™
(732) 792-1108
www.junkitz.com

K & Company
(888) 244-2083
www.kandcompany.com

Kangaroo & Joey®, Inc.
(800) 646-8065
www.kangarooandjoey.com

Karen Foster Design
(801) 451-9779
www.karenfosterdesign.com

KI Memories
(972) 243-5595
www.kimemories.com

Krylon®
(216) 566-200
www.krylon.com

Lazar Studiowerx, Inc.
(866) 478-9379
www.lazarstudiowerx.com

Li'l Davis Designs
(949) 838-0344
www.lildavisdesigns.com

M & J Trimming
(800) 9-MJTRIM
www.mjtrim.com

Magenta Rubber Stamps
(800) 565-5254
www.magentastyle.com

Magic Mesh
(651) 345-6374
www.magicmesh.com

Magic Scraps™
(972) 238-1838
www.magicscraps.com

Making Memories
(800) 286-5263
www.makingmemories.com

Maya Road, LLC
(214) 488-3279
www.mayaroad.com

May Arts
(800) 442-3950
www.mayarts.com

me & my BiG ideas®
(949) 883-2065
www.meandmybigideas.com

Melissa Frances.
(905) 686-9031
www.melissafrances.com

Source Guide

Michaels® Arts & Crafts
(800) 642-4235
www.michaels.com

Midwestern Home Products- no contact info

Moonshine Design
(801) 397-3997
www.moonshinedsgn.com

Mustard Moon™
(408) 299-8542
www.mustardmoon.com

My Mind's Eye™, Inc.
(800) 665-5116
www.frame-ups.com

Nunn Design
(360) 379-3557
www.nunndesign.com

Paper Adventures®
(800) 525-3196
www.paperadventures.com

Paper Company, The/ANW Crestwood
(800) 525-3196
www.anwcrestwood.com

Pebbles Inc.
(801) 224-1857
www.pebblesinc.com

Plaid Enterprises, Inc.
(800) 842-4197
www.plaidonline.com

PM designs
(888) 595-2887
www.designsbypm.com

Postmodern Design
(405) 321-3176
www.stampdiva.com

Prima Marketing, Inc.
(909) 627-5532
www.mulberrypaperflowers.com

Provo Craft®
(888) 577-3545
www.provocraft.com

PSX Design™
(800) 782-6748
www.psxdesign.com

Queen & Co.
(858) 485-5132
www.queenandcompany.com

QuicKutz, Inc.
(801) 765-1144
www.quickutz.com

Ranger Industries, Inc.
(800) 244-2211
www.rangerink.com

Reminisce Papers
(319) 358-9777
www.shopreminisce.com

Robin's Nest Press, The
(435) 789-5387
robins@sbnet.com

Rocky Mountain Scrapbook Co.
(801) 785-9695
www.rmscrapbook.com

Rubba Dub Dub
(707) 748-0929
www.artsanctum.com

Rubber Stampede
(800) 423-4135
www.deltacrafts.com

Rusty Pickle
(801) 746-1045
www.rustypickle.com

Saunders
(207) 685-3385
www.saunders-usa.com

Scenic Route Paper Co.
(801) 785-0761
www.scenicroutepaper.com

Scrapworks, LLC
(801) 363-1010
www.scrapworks.com

SEI, Inc.
(800) 333-3279
www.shopsei.com

Sizzix®
(866) 742-4447
www.sizzix.com

Spellbinders™ Paper Arts, LLC
(888) 547-0400
www.spellbinders.us

Stampendous!®
(800) 869-0474
www.stampendous.com

Stamping Station™
(801) 444-3828
www.stampingstation.com

Sticker Studio™
(208) 322-2465
www.stickerstudio.com

Target
www.target.com

Technique Tuesday, LLC
(503) 644-4073
www.techniquetuesday.com

Tsukineko®, Inc.
(800) 769-6633
www.tsukineko.com

Urban Lily- no contact info

Wal-Mart Stores, Inc.
(800) WALMART
www.walmart.com

Walnut Hollow® Farm, Inc.
(800) 950-5101
www.walnuthollow.com

Wendi Speciale Designs
www.wendispeciale.com

Wrights® Ribbon Accents
(877) 597-4448
www.wrights.com

Index

Artist Index

Discover more awesome uses for leftover page supplies with these great titles from Memory Makers Books!

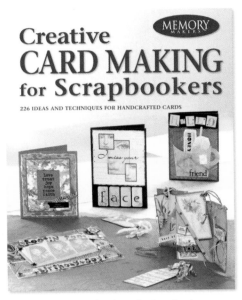

Creative Card Making for Scrapbookers
ISBN-13: 978-1-892127-43-3,
ISBN-10: 1-89212-743-1,
paperback, 128 pgs., #33008

Making Gift Scrapbooks in a Snap
ISBN-13: 978-1892127-36-5,
ISBN-10: 1-89212-736-9,
paperback, 96 pgs., #32994

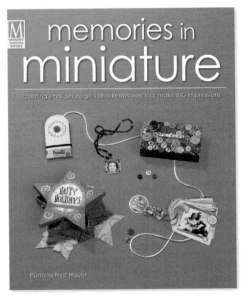

Memories in Miniature
ISBN-13: 978-1-892127-50-1,
ISBN-10: 1-89212-750-4,
paperback, 96 pgs., #33266

Scrapbook Memorabilia
ISBN-13: 978-1-892127-76-1,
ISBN-10: 1-89212-776-8,
paperback, 96 pgs., #Z0011